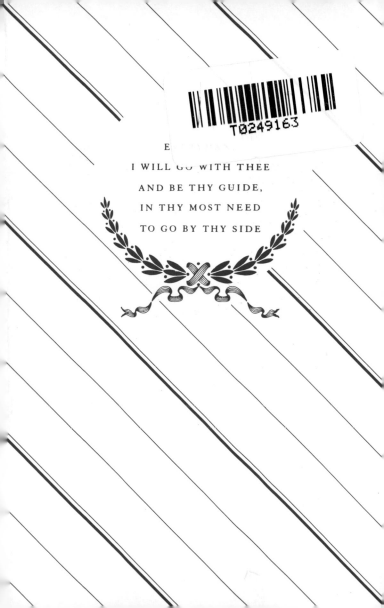

E
I WILL GO WITH THEE
AND BE THY GUIDE,
IN THY MOST NEED
TO GO BY THY SIDE

EVERYMAN'S LIBRARY
POCKET POETS

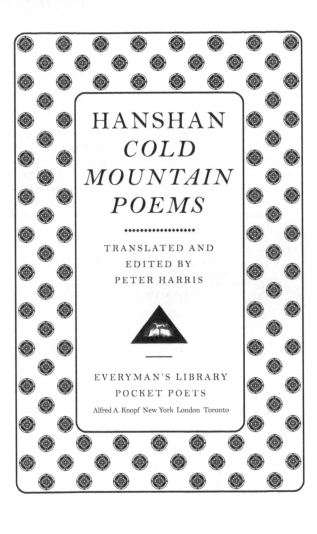

# HANSHAN
## *COLD*
## *MOUNTAIN*
## *POEMS*

••••••••••••••••••

TRANSLATED AND
EDITED BY
PETER HARRIS

EVERYMAN'S LIBRARY
POCKET POETS

Alfred A. Knopf  New York  London  Toronto

THIS IS A BORZOI BOOK
PUBLISHED BY ALFRED A. KNOPF

This selection by Peter Harris first published in
Everyman's Library, 2024
Copyright © 2024 by Everyman's Library
English translation copyright © 2024 by Peter Harris

everymanslibrary.com
www.everymanslibrary.co.uk

ISBN 978-1-101-90845-7 (US)
978-1-84159-833-8 (UK)

A CIP catalogue record for this book is available from the
British Library

Typography by Peter B. Willberg

Typeset in the UK by Input Data Services, Bridgwater, Somerset

Printed and bound in Germany
by GGP Media GmbH, Pössneck

# CONTENTS

## XIV. ON HANSHAN'S POEMS

# PREFACE

Hanshan, which means Cold Mountain in English, was traditionally thought to be a reclusive seventh-century Buddhist monk who lived on Tiantai, a mountain range in Zhejiang province of southeast China.

An early Chinese account of Hanshan portrays him as a wayward figure living in seclusion near a Tiantai temple called Guoqing, where he had a friend called Shide or Foundling who worked in the temple kitchen. According to this account Hanshan went around writing his poems on bamboos, cliffs and walls. The account is supposed to have been written by a seventh-century Tang dynasty official who met Hanshan at Guoqing temple and had a local monk go out and write down all his poems. The sinologist Victor Mair has suggested that this local monk, Daoqiao, may have been the author of most of the poems himself.

Doubts have been cast on the authenticity of both this early account and its putative author. In line with these doubts, others have dated Hanshan later, one well-established view being that his life spanned the late eighth and early ninth centuries BCE.

Otherwise what little we know about Hanshan comes from the poems themselves. Some 313 of them have survived, with a number of others presumed lost. (In one poem there's mention of six hundred poems.) The extant poems are not by any means internally consistent. But at a stretch they can be taken to describe someone who grew up in a farming family, then left home to travel around China, perhaps serving for a while as a government official, before eventually settling as a Buddhist monk on Tiantai. There he lived for many decades and died a very old man. He called the place he chose to live in Cold Mountain, Cold Cliff or Cinnabar Hill.

In several poems Hanshan refers to a wife and children, all unnamed. But he seems to have ended up alone and reliant on the occasional companionship of a few locals, most of whom died before he did. These included Foundling and another monk, Fenggan (Broad Shield), both of whom are closely associated with Hanshan but are, in fact, only mentioned in his poems once.

As the great translator Arthur Waley once remarked, in the Hanshan poems 'Cold Mountain is often the name of a state of mind rather than a locality' – the state of mind being the peace that comes from tranquil and enlightened understanding. In many instances Hanshan's poems merge state of mind and locality into one.

One reason Hanshan's poems lack consistency is that they were almost certainly written by more than one person. One linguist has claimed on the basis of the poems' use of rhymes that they consisted of work by two people, one of them active during the early part of the Tang dynasty (618–907 CE) or even earlier, and another writing towards the end of the Tang.

18

Others have gone further, even suggesting that the Hanshan collection is no more than that – a collection or anthology of poems, many of them sharing a Zen-like approach to life, that derives from a number of different hands over some three centuries.

The author or authors of the Hanshan poems are routinely considered to be a man or men, but if the Hanshan corpus were indeed an anthology there would be no reason to exclude women from those contributing to it. Buddhist nuns were a feature of Tang society, as were women writers, though the latter were under-appreciated in what was very much a male-oriented society.

Hanshan's poems are notable for being written in the vernacular rather than classical Chinese. In terms of style and content they vary considerably. Taking the order in which the 313 or so extant poems are customarily arranged, a fair number of the earlier poems have a bluff, personal quality to them that some of the later, more elaborate poems lack. Later poems also include a relatively high proportion of more explicitly Buddhist teachings and musings.

But this is a very rough-and-ready assessment, for while they are fairly consistent in format – the great majority are eight-line poems with five characters per line – the Hanshan poems cover a broad spectrum of styles and themes. Some of these are typical of the poetry of the times, others more idiosyncratic. They range from evocative portrayals of mountain scenes to reflections on the transience of life, and from accounts of tranquillity to descriptions of worry and discomfort. They also include fairytale vignettes, blunt admonitions and plain doggerel.

In China Hanshan has never been part of the pantheon of great poets such as Du Fu, Li Bai and Wang Wei. But he long held a respected position as a Buddhist poet with Zen leanings, not only in China and Japan but also in Korea and Vietnam. In the English-speaking world he came to fame much more recently, in the 1950s, when Arthur Waley lent his work respectability by translating some of his poems for *Encounter* magazine. More importantly, perhaps, Hanshan was adopted by the Beat Generation. Gary Snyder translated a selection of his poems, and Jack Kerouac dedicated *The Dharma Bums* to Hanshan. Hanshan was perceived to be a cool Zen figure whose lifestyle and philosophy went wonderfully well with Beat Generation ideals.

Since then Hanshan has been translated in whole or in part a number of times (see the Note at the end for other translations) and retained a loyal following in the English-speaking world. Learned editions of his work by modern Japanese and Chinese scholars have also helped make him more accessible to contemporary east Asian audiences.

For this Pocket Poets edition I have selected some two-thirds of the Hanshan poems for translation, leaving out a number that contain obscure historical references, dwell on Buddhist themes in a repetitive way, or otherwise make for awkward reading today. I have also taken the liberty of dividing the poems into different topics, fourteen in all. In this way you can, I hope, enjoy all the poems on living in seclusion, say, in one section, and all the poems on the transience of life in another, rather than stumbling on such topics by chance.

The topics are by no means watertight, for many of the poems manage to touch on more than one theme in a single eight lines. But they can perhaps serve as helpful signposts into poems that still offer insights, comfort and delight in today's turbulent world, well over a millennium after they were first written.

Peter Harris

# I. THE SECLUDED LIFE

1.

I chose a place to live by layered cliffs
on a path for birds without any human tracks.
What's out there, where the courtyard ends? –
white clouds wrapped around dark rocks.
During the several years I've been living here
I've watched each winter turning into spring.
Tell the wealthy with their bells and bronzes
there's nothing at all to gain from empty fame.

2.

It's such a delight, the road to Cold Mountain
and yet there isn't a trace of horse or cart.
It's hard to recall how it winds from gorge to gorge
or know the number of folds in the teetering cliffs.
Hundreds of different grasses drip with dew;
winds sigh among the unchanging pines.
At this point, lost for a way ahead
I ask my shadow, 'Where do we go from here?'

3.

I love living the life of a recluse
cut off from the hustle of the world.
I've trodden grass to make three paths to my door;
the clouds are my neighbours, wherever I look up.
The birds are here to help with the sound of song
but there's no one around to ask about the dharma.
Today the Bodhi tree is making
the spring season last several years.

Dharma here is Buddhist teaching. The tree Hanshan
mentions, *suopo*, seems to be the sal tree, the Indian tree
often thought to be the Bodhi or 'awakening' tree the
Buddha sat under.

4.

I should stick to my zither and my books –
what's the use of salary or rank?
I've put aside the carriage, as my good wife urged;
my devoted son is here to drive the cart.
Breezes blow on the ground where we sun the grain
and our fishpond is full to overflowing.
I often contemplate the wren
sitting there at rest on a single branch.

The zither is the *qin*.

5.

People ask the way to Cold Mountain
but the path there doesn't get through.
Even in summer the ice lingers on
and mists obscure the emerging sun.
So how did someone like myself make it here?
My heart and mind are not the same as yours.
If you had a heart and mind like mine
you'd be able to get there too.

Here and later *xin*, heart, is rendered as heart and mind, since
the heart was believed to be the seat of thinking.

6.

Heaven produced a tree a hundred feet high
which was cut up into lengthy pieces of wood.
What a shame these timbers good for beams
were cast aside into a shadowy gully.
Many years on they've stayed sturdy at heart
though over time their bark's been worn away.
Some knowing person will carry them off –
they'll still be fit for propping up a stable.

7.

My parents have left me plenty to look after –
I've no desire for others' gardens and fields.
Clickety-clack, my wife works at her loom
among the children babbling as they play.
Clapping away, I urge the blossoms to dance,
listen to the birdsong, chin in hand.
Who comes to admire all this? –
sometimes a woodcutter passes by.

8.

My home lies beneath the green cliffs,
the weeds in my courtyard left uncut.
New creepers hang down intertwined
over ancient rocks that rise up sheer.
Monkeys pick the mountain fruit, and egrets
slip the fish in the pond into their bills.
With a chapter or two of an immortal's work
I sit under a tree, murmuring as I read.

'an immortal's work': a general term for a Daoist classic
of some kind.
'murmuring': books were customarily read aloud.

9.

The New Year comes to replace a sad year past;
spring is here and things are looking fresh.
Mountain blossoms smile on the green streams;
trees on the cliffside dance in the deep blue mist.
Happy as always, the butterflies and bees,
the birds and fishes an even greater delight.
The feeling of being with friends stays with me
and until dawn comes I can't get to sleep.

10.

If you want a place for a settled life,
Cold Mountain can take care of you for ever.
Under shadowy pines blown by a light breeze –
which sound even better close at hand –
a man with white-flecked hair murmurs as he reads
the works of the Yellow Emperor and Master Lao.
These ten years there's been no going back for him –
he's forgotten the road he took here when he came.

'the Yellow Emperor and Master Lao': founding figures of
an early Daoist school of learning. Master Lao (Lao zi) was
author of the Daoist classic *Dao de jing*.

11.

There's a master who dines on rosy clouds,
his dwelling place beyond the reach of the world.
I'd say that it's a truly refreshing place
where summer heat is like the autumn cool
and shady mountain streams go trickling on
as breezes sigh within the lofty pines.
If you sit among them for half a day
you'll forget a century of sorrows.

12.

Pull hard on the oars of your lightweight boat,
ride your swiftly galloping horse with skill,
but still you won't succeed in reaching my home,
for by my reckoning it's in the darkest of wilds,
among the mountain caves and plunging cliffs,
clouds and thunder rolling through the day.
I'm not the Lord Confucius, and so
there's no one here to help you on your way.

Confucius seems an unlikely saviour here. Perhaps there's a
copying error, and the person Hanshan really refers to
is Fuqiu, whose written name is like Kong Qiu (Confucius).
Fuqiu was an early Daoist who helped an immortal climb
a mountain.

13.

There's a bird decked out in many colours,
there on the tung tree eating bamboo fruit.
It moves in a stately way, as if performing a ritual,
and sings sweetly with a perfect pitch.
It arrived yesterday by means unknown,
appearing before us for just this short time.
When it hears the strains of strings and song
it dances about, happy for the day.

The bird seems to be a *feng* or phoenix, an auspicious creature
that appears only to sages and great rulers.

14.

I live in a thatched house in the wilds
where horses and carts seldom come to the gate.
Throughout the gloom of the forest birds gather;
fish forever hide in the broad stream.
I take the children to pick the mountain fruit
and join my wife in hoeing the paddy fields.
What is there inside our house? —
nothing but a bed holding some books.

15.

When you climb the road to Cold Mountain
the mountain path stretches out endlessly –
its gorges long, the rocks in tumbled heaps,
its spacious streams enmeshed with wild grass.
The moss is slippery, but not from rain;
it isn't wind that makes the sounds in the pines.
Who can disentangle themselves from the world
and join me to sit among the white clouds?

16.

Amidst the high mountains in white clouds
and the green water's rippling waves
fishermen frequently sing their songs
as they pull away at their oars.
I can't listen to their every sound –
they bring on too many sad thoughts.
'Who says the sparrow has no beak? –
see how it pecks its way into my house.'

'Who says the sparrow . . .': lines from the old *Classic of Songs*,
interpreted as referring to an action – like the fisherman's
singing, perhaps? – that unwittingly disturbs you.

17.

Hidden away, the Cold Mountain road;
isolated, the cold banks of the stream.
There's often the chattering of the birds
but otherwise I'm entirely alone.
The blustery wind blows in my face;
flurrying snowflakes settle on me in heaps.
Day after day I don't see the sun,
year in year out I haven't known the spring.

18.

I dwell alone beneath the tiered cliffs,
billowing clouds clustering through the day.
But even though it's gloomy inside the house
my heart and mind are not in the least disturbed.
In my dreams I wander through the Golden Gates,
my soul returning across the Stone Bridge.
I've thrown away whatever troubles me –
the tap-tap of a gourd hung in the trees.

The Golden Gates and Stone Bridge were two renowned
sights on or near Tiantai. The Stone Bridge was a high,
narrow path. The tapping gourd was a gourd once given as
a cup to a mountain recluse. He hung the gourd on a nearby
tree, but its tapping so annoyed him that he threw it away.

19.

My heart and mind are like the autumn moon,
pure and perfectly clear in a dark green pool,
fit to be compared with nothing else –
tell me, how can I explain?


20.

If you stay silent and never say a word
what will those who come after you have to relate?
If you hide yourself away in the forested wilds
how will the light of your wisdom ever emerge?
Getting decrepit doesn't help your circulation;
wind and frost make you sick and die in your prime.
Plough a stony field with an ox of clay
and you will never enjoy a harvest day.

21.

How bitterly cold the mountains have been,
not just this year, but since long ago –
layered peaks forever freezing the snow,
shadowy forests frequently spitting mist.
Grasses grow only after the Grain is in Beard;
leaves fall even before the Autumn Begins.
Here's a visitor who's completely lost,
peering up, unable to see the sky.

Grain in Beard, Autumn Begins: two stages of the old
agricultural calendar, early and late summer respectively.

22.

I selected this secluded spot to live in
on Tiantai, about which there's nothing more to say.
Apes cry out and the mist in the gorge is chill;
mountain shades come up to my grassy gate.
I break off leaves to thatch my home in the pines;
for a pond I draw water from a mountain spring.
My feelings no longer disturbed by the world's
    affairs,
I gather bracken fern in my final years.

Tiantai was the mountain in Zhejiang province where
Hanshan made a home.

23.

Clear, the spring waters of the high blue stream;
Pale, the moonlight over Cold Mountain.
In the stillness I see that my spirit innately
    knows –
I gaze into emptiness, the world ever more calm.


24.

Graceful streams line the layered mountains,
their faded blues locked in a pink haze.
My light scarf wet, brushed by the mist,
my straw raincoat soaked by the dew,
my feet clad in travellers' sandals
and an old cane walking stick in hand,
I gaze out beyond the dusty world –
what is it then, the realm of dreams?


The realm of dreams is the illusory world we inhabit
day to day.

25.

My scrolls are filled with verses by capable poets;
my jug overflows with the clear wine called 'divine'.
Out walking I like to keep an eye on the calves;
back home I sit with scroll and jug at my side.
Frost and dew seep into my thatched eaves;
moonlight shines through windows of broken jars.
At this time I sip at a cup or two,
chanting several poems as I do.

Poor people made small round windows out of broken jars.

26.

The farmers get away from the summer heat –
who's joining them to enjoy a measure of wine?
They've laid out heaps of mountain fruit
and spread out cups of wine all around.
Seated on matting made of reeds
we dine off plates made of banana leaf.
As we sit drunk, our cheeks propped on our hands,
Mount Meru shrinks into a little pellet.

To Buddhists, Mount Meru was a mighty sacred mountain,
centre of the universe.

27.

If the bird calls are too touching to bear
I take a rest in my thatched retreat
where cherries and peaches glisten red
and willows cascade in disarray.
The morning sun swallows the dark cliffs;
scattered clouds freshen the deep green lake.
Who's to know you can leave the dusty world
and drive your cart up Cold Mountain's south side?

28.

Yesterday, how quiet and soothing it was –
a delight to be there in the open space,
a path through peaches and plums up above,
below an island grown over with sweet flag,
and in a cottage a fine-looking woman
dressed in silk and kingfisher feathers.
Happening on her I wanted to call to her
but I was at a loss for words.

29.

In the western mountains a late crimson sun
casts its shimmering rays on grasses and trees,
among them places sunk into murky shadow,
their creepers intertwined among the pines.
Crouching tigers abound in their midst;
if they see me their hackles will rise for a chase.
I don't have the smallest knife to hand
so I'm feeling frightened – and why not?

30.

Many are the mysteries of Cold Mountain –
those that climb it are all in constant awe.
The moon shines on crystal-clear streams;
the wind blows through whispering grasses.
On faded plum trees snow forms like blossoms;
clouds take the guise of leaves on stumps of trees.
If you run into rain everything comes alive
but you can't get through unless the skies are clear.

Hanshan's modern editor Xiang Chu thinks lines five and six
of this poem are especially fine.

31.

Before the woods emerged, a tree appeared –
I'd estimate it's more than twice their age.
Its roots adapted to a changing landscape;
its leaves came and went with the wind and frost.
Everyone laughs that its outside's worn away
without caring about its fine inner markings.
Its bark has completely peeled away
leaving only the true core behind.

32.

I have lived on Cold Mountain
for countless ages past,
hiding in the wilds as fate ordains,
idly gazing at a free-floating world.
No one gets as far as these cold cliffs,
forever wrapped in the white clouds.
Sparse grasses serve as my couch;
the deep blue sky is my counterpane.
It's a joy to pillow my head on a rock
as earth and sky go through their changes.

33.

A prodigious thing, Cold Mountain,
its white clouds carelessly slipping ever by.
The cries of monkeys carry to the road;
a tiger's roar reaches the outside world.
Walking alone, my feet are firm on the rocks;
as I recite verse, the creepers are good to climb,
amid the clear sighs of wind in the pines
and the sounds of birds calling.

34.

Taking life easy I visit an eminent monk
in the countless layers of misty mountains.
The master himself points to my path home,
lit by the hanging lamp of the moon.

35.

I make my leisurely way up to Hua Peak,
a bright sun glistening in the dawn light.
Everywhere in the clear heavens
white clouds and cranes go soaring by.

Huading or Hua Peak is the name of the highest peak of
Mount Tiantai.

36.

Hanshan has a dwelling
with no divisions inside.
Six doors open out to left and right,
the blue of the sky visible from the hall.
Every room is completely empty,
its east wall across from its west wall
with not a single thing in between
for anyone to be concerned about.
When it's cold he lights a modest fire,
cooking vegetables if he's hungry.
He doesn't do as the old farmers do,
building up fields and houses,
making karma that lands them in hell
which they'll never leave once there.
Give this some careful thought
and you'll know the principles of life.

Karma: the consequences of past actions on future
fate or lives.

37.

Since withdrawing to Cold Mountain
I've sustained myself with mountain fruits.
What is there to be sad about in life
as I go with my destiny in this world?
The days and months are like a passing stream;
time goes by in a flash, a flintstone's spark.
Let the earth and sky transform themselves;
I'm content to sit among the cliffs.

Destiny here and later is *yuan*, a Chinese word referring to the
conditions that predetermine our lives.

38.

My aim is steadfast – you should know
that it isn't just a mat you can bundle up.
As I stroll into the mountain forest
and rest on my own on a large flat rock
a skilled debater comes and urges me
to take forthwith the gold and jade of office.
But like drilling into a wall to plant brambles
there'd be nothing to gain from doing so.

'My mind is not a stone, it can't be rolled about; my mind is
not a mat, it can't be rolled up' are lines in the early *Classic of
Songs*. The skilled debater is a court official offering Hanshan
a job. Drilling into a wall to plant brambles is a saying from
the Daoist classic *Zhuang zi*. It means interfering officiously
and without any point.

39.

This place where I rest and roam about
has hidden mysteries which are hard to describe.
Creepers move on their own without a breeze;
the bamboo's always hazy though there's no mist.
The green valley stream sounds like someone
        sobbing;
on the mountains clouds suddenly come together.
Sitting in my hut it gets to be midday
before I feel the warmth of the sun.

40.

I remember the places I went to
travelling round the world's famous sites.
Delighting in mountains I climbed incredibly high;
loving the waters I sailed in countless boats.
I saw off travellers at Lute Gorge,
took my zither to Parrot Island.
How would I know I'd end up under the pines
hugging my knees in the chilly wind?

Lute Gorge hasn't been identified. Parrot Island is on the
Yangzi River. The lute is the *pipa* and the zither is the *qin*.

41.

Last spring with the singing of the birds
was a time when I thought about my brothers.
This autumn as the chrysanthemums fade
is a time to think of next year's new growth.
The clear stream sounds with countless sobs;
yellow clouds lie level on every side.
It's distressing that within my lifetime
I'm broken-hearted remembering Xianyang.

The old name Xianyang refers to the Tang capital Chang'an.
Hanshan may have been broken-hearted at the memory of
the capital because of its destruction by the great An Lushan
rebellion in the mid-eighth century.

42.

What a shame – this century-old house
is collapsing to left and right,
its walls completely in pieces,
its timbers scattered around.
Every single tile has fallen off –
it's too decayed to be lived in.
If a strong wind suddenly blows it down
it'll end up being hard to rebuild.

Hanshan commonly refers to a lifetime being a century long.
So perhaps the house is Hanshan himself.

43.

I have a body and I have no body;
there is a self and there is not a self.
I was deep in thought on these matters,
seated for a long time against a cliff.
The green grass grew between my feet
and red dust dropped down on my head.
I saw common folk laying out wine and fruit
as they would in front of a body on a bier.

The first two lines are similar to lines in the *Nirvana Sutra*,
the sacred text telling of the Buddha before he died.

44.

Yesterday I saw some trees by the riverside
in a state of decay that can't be described.
Two or three trunks were still standing,
scarred by the countless cuts of axe blades.
Frost had bitten into the few withered leaves
and water lapped across the rotten roots.
That's how it is, wherever there is life —
it's no use resenting heaven and earth.

45.

How many autumns have I spent on Cold Mountain,
singing songs by myself, not a sorrow in the world.
My wicker gate's not closed – it's always secluded,
a gushing spring's sweet waters flowing on and on.
A clay pot bubbles on the earth stove in my cave;
my cup smells of froth from pine-pollen cypress tea.
If I'm hungry I take a grain of the elixir of life;
tranquil in heart and mind, I lean against a rock.

The elixir of life here is the all-purpose curative *agada*. Some
versions of this poem do not include the four middle lines.

46.

Cinnabar Hill soars as high as the clouds;
five peaks in the void look down from afar.
Wild Goose Pagoda pushes through dark crags
and the old Zen temple rises into a rainbow.
Pine leaves flutter on the elegant Red Wall;
mist spurts at mid-level, the immortals' path a haze.
Against the blue you see countless lofty mountains,
wistaria intertwined in connecting valleys.

Cinnabar Hill is another name for Mount Tiantai; Red Wall is
the name of a nearby peak. The name Wild Goose Pagoda was
often used to mean a Buddhist temple.

47.

A host of stars is spread in the late moonlight,
the cliffs lit by a single lamp, the sinking moon,
its splendour perfect and unpolished
hanging in the sky – my heart and mind.

48.

An ancient's footprints on a primeval rock –
an empty spot in front of towering cliffs.
When the moon shines, it's always crystal clear;
don't bother searching or asking the direction.

49.

I watch the blue stream in the valley ahead
or sit on a boulder by the side of the cliff,
my heart and mind a solitary cloud, relying on
     nothing –
what's there to seek in the distant affairs of the
     world?

50.

Tiantai is where I live, and where thick mist
keeps visitors away from the path through the
     clouds.
Deep in the soaring peaks I can hide
in rocky towers among countless deep-set gullies.
I walk them wearing birch-bark scarf and clogs,
winding upwards in my cloth gown, goosefoot
     stick in hand.
I'm conscious that this floating life is an illusion –
how fine it is to be happy and roaming free.

51.

Since coming to this realm of Tiantai
I've lived through quite a few winters and springs.
Mountains and rivers don't change, but of course
     people age
and I've seen a fair number from later generations.

52.

Yesterday rambling on the mountaintops
I peered down a thousand-foot precipice.
By the perilous drop stood a single tree
splayed by the wind into two limbs.
These had withered in the blasting rain,
turned to dirt under the baking sun.
Ah, to see such a resplendent thing
reduced now to an accumulation of ash.

Poem number 51 is also attributed to Hanshan's
companion Shide.

53.

Living free and easy in the white clouds
a mountain isn't something you'd ever buy.
You need a walking stick on the dangerous slopes,
grasping at creepers to climb up perilous heights.
The gully pines are forever a kingfisher green;
stones are naturally mottled by the streams.
You are separated from your friends
but spring brings the songs of the birds.

Buying a mountain: the respected early Buddhist monk Zhi
Dun tried to buy a mountain to retire to.

54.

I'm content with the way I've led my life
amongst the misty creepers and rocky caves,
my untamed feelings quite open and free,
my lasting companions the easygoing white clouds.
There are paths here, but they don't lead to the
    world;
having no heart and mind, what is there to climb?
I sit on a bed of stone in the lonely night,
a round moon rising over Cold Mountain.

55.

If you look at the summit of Tiantai,
it stands high above all the other mountains.
Through pine and bamboo a sweet breeze blows;
sea tides come and go as the moon appears.
As I gaze down to the dark edge of the mountain
I talk about mysteries among the white clouds.
Mountain and water set my feelings free –
I aim to be like the followers of the Way.

56.

In our times people search for a path in the clouds
but the path in the clouds doesn't leave a trace.
The high mountains are full of precipices;
the broad ravines are generally rough-hewn.
Blue cliffs rise up before and behind you;
white clouds float to east and west.
If you want to know where the path in the clouds is,
the path in the clouds is in the emptiness.

57.

Hanshan stays in his retreat
cut off from incidental passers-by.
Sometimes he comes across forest birds
and together they sing a mountain song.
Sacred grasses grow across the gorges
and old pines curl up to the heights.
You can see him, free of all concerns,
resting in a corner of a cliff.

58.

I long for the pleasures of the mountains –
free of care, of anything to depend on,
every day sustaining this ageing frame
with idle thoughts of having nothing to do.
Sometimes I leaf through an old Buddhist sutra
and frequently I climb up a stone walkway,
there to peer down a thousand-foot cliff
while the clouds linger overhead.
The winter moon gives out a frosty light;
I am like a solitary crane in flight.

59.

So estimable a thing, this famous mountain,
not to be compared with other treasures.
The moon in the pines shines with a frosty light;
streak upon streak, the pinks of the clouds rise up.
Layered hills in clusters circle around,
twisting and turning, mile after endless mile.
The streams in the gorges run quiet and clear
and my contentment knows no bounds.

60.

It towers beyond the firmament –
the path there soaring into the clouds
by a waterfall cascading thousands of feet,
spread out like a length of white silk.
There's a cave below for resting the heart and mind,
across it a bridge to a place that decides your fate.
Tiantai with its all-surpassing name
keeps a mighty watch on the world.

The bridge may be the Stone Bridge leading to the immortals'
tree mentioned elsewhere.

61.

I sit on a large flat stone
by a cool mountain stream,
quietly enjoying its particular beauty,
half-hidden by mist on the bare cliff.
I'm happy to stay in this restful place
as sunset deepens the shadows of the trees.
When I look into my heart and mind
lotuses are growing out of the mire.

62.

When recluses escape from the world
many of them sleep within the mountains
by dark vines that spread out one by one
and blue streams that murmur on and on.
They're untroubled and contented
and eternally at ease with themselves,
unsullied by the world's affairs,
pure in heart and mind like the white lotus.

63.

Cold Cliff is buried away, and that's fine –
no one comes along this way.
White clouds float idly by the high peaks;
a lone monkey cries from the dark crags.
And what is it that's dear to me? –
doing as I intend, ageing as it suits me.
My looks change with the passing seasons
but the pearl in my heart and mind stays secure.

Cold Cliff was another name for Cold Mountain.

64.

I sit quietly on my own in front of the cliff,
a full moon lighting up the sky.
Among the countless shadows
the moon of itself does not shine.
The vacant spirit, clear in itself,
holds an empty mystery.
When it's pointed out, you see its moon –
the moon as the focus of heart and mind.

65.

Today I am seated in front of a cliff;
after I've sat for some time the mist disperses.
The clear mountain stream is cold;
blue crags soar thousands of feet.
By day white clouds cast silent shadows;
at night-time moonbeams float in the air.
I'm free of the dust of worldly care –
nothing is left to vex my heart and mind.

66.

Hundreds of clouds among innumerable streams
and somebody taking life easy in their midst.
During the day I roam the dark green mountains;
at night I return to sleep below the cliffs.
Speedily the seasons come and go;
I am serene, without any worldly ties.
It's such a delight to depend on nothing at all,
placid like a river in the autumn.

67.

High, high up on the mountain peak
I look at endless expanses all around.
I sit here alone and nobody knows;
cold spring water reflects the solitary moon.
What's within the water isn't the moon;
the moon is just up there in the dark sky.
I've been chanting this song
and what's within the song isn't Zen.

68.

Cold Mountain is nothing but white clouds
quietly cutting off the dusty world.
A recluse is seated on a straw mat
under the single lamp of a full moon.
His bed of stone overlooks a blue pond;
his everyday neighbours are tigers and deer.
He longs to dwell in the joy of seclusion
forever beyond the things of this world.

69.

I rest and roam about below Cold Cliff,
marvelling at its wonders,
gathering mountain vegetables in my basket,
picking fruit to take back in my pannier.
In my lowly home, rushes spread as a seat,
I make a meal of purple mushrooms,
washing my cup and bowl in a clear pond
and cooking up a mixture of rice and gruel.
Then I sit in the sun wrapped in a fur gown,
casually reading the work of the old poets.

70.

I've been wanting to go to the east cliff
for I don't know how many years.
Yesterday I clambered up its creepers
but half-way up I was hit by wind and mist.
The path was so narrow my clothes got in the way
and my shoes wouldn't move, stuck with moss.
So I stopped under this sweet olive tree
and fell asleep pillowed in white clouds.

71.

Nobody reaches
the road to Cold Mountain.
Those that can travel it
are acclaimed as a Buddha.
Cicadas sing here
but crows don't caw.
Yellow leaves fall;
white clouds sweep by.
Rocks are piled up
and the mountain is hidden.
I sit on my own,
known as a fine teacher;
but look with care –
I bear no visible signs.

'acclaimed as a Buddha': literally, acclaimed with ten
titles – the ten honorific titles given to the Buddha. 'visible
signs': there are supposed to be various external signs of
Buddhahood, but Hanshan has none of them.

72.

Cold Mountain is chilly
and ice frosts over the rocks,
hiding the green of the mountain,
showing the white of the snow.
The sun begins to shine
and after a while it thaws.
From then on it's warm
and this old visitor's revived.


73.

I live in the mountains
and no one knows me.
Among the white clouds
it's always quiet and still.

74.

Cold Mountain's buried away –
that suits my heart and mind.
It has pure white rocks
but there isn't any gold.
The echoes of spring water
are like Bo Ya playing the zither;
here is a Zhong Ziqi
to appreciate the sound.

Long ago Bo Ya was an outstanding zither (*qin*) player. Only
one listener, Zhong Ziqi, truly appreciated his music. As he
listens to the sound of the spring water Hanshan compares
himself to Zhong Ziqi.

## II. WORRIES, MELANCHOLY
   AND STRIFE

75.

What do the young have to be worried about?
They're worried to see the hair on their temples
    turn white.
And why are they worried about it turning white?
They're worried to see the days press
    relentlessly on.
They'll move to a dwelling that faces Mount Tai
or be sent to care for a grave on Mount Mang.
How difficult it is to say these words,
words that bring distress to an old man.

Mount Tai, one of China's five sacred mountains, was
associated with the spirits of the dead and hell. Mount
Mang near the old capital Luoyang was the site of an old
burial ground.

76.

I've heard it said that worries are hard to dispel.
As I see it, there's no truth to these words.
Yet yesterday I sent my worries packing
only for them to grip me again today.
The month may end but worries are hard to end;
when the year is new, worries renew themselves too.
Who's to know that my broad-brimmed rattan hat
hides someone who's always been a worrier?

77.

This mountain visitor's sad in heart and mind
and often sighs at the passing of the years.
He wears himself out gathering mushrooms and
    roots
but clearing the land won't make him an immortal.
The clouds start rolling back from the spacious
    yard;
the woods are bright with the light of the just-full
    moon.
If he doesn't go back, what is he to do? –
the sweet olive trees are pressing him to stay.

Eating certain mushrooms and roots was thought to promote
long life. An old lament associated sweet olive trees (*gui*,
which may also refer to cinnamon) with lingering in a
mountain fastness.

78.

There is someone     on the mountain slope
where the clouds are lifting     fringed with rosy light
who holds a bouquet     he would like to send
but the road stretches far     and is hard to travel –
despondent in heart and mind     and beset by misgivings
he stands alone     faithful and pure.

There are several versions of this poem, which is written in
the style of the old *Songs of South*, with mid-line breaks.

79.

It's a troubling business, serving as an official,
given the world's affairs take many forms.
You can't yet cast aside the common crowd
and so go asking after those you know,
yesterday mourning the death of Xu Five,
today seeing off the funeral of Liu Three.
The whole day there's no rest to be had,
leaving you distraught in heart and mind.

The fictitious names Xu Five and Liu Three both consist of a
surname and a birth-order number. So Mr Xu was born fifth
in his family, and Mr Liu third. Birth-order numbers were in
common use at the time.

80.

As I sit alone I'm often cast down
with such feelings of melancholy.
Mid-level clouds curl around the mountain;
wind whistles from the mouth of a gorge.
As monkeys climb the trees they softly sway;
birds entering the forest chirrup away.
Time presses on – the hair on my temples fades;
year's end brings the lost hopes of age.

81.

Sad to say, I am poor and sick,
cut off from my relatives and friends.
For ages there's been no rice in the storage jar
and the rice cooker is frequently lined with dust.
My thatched hut doesn't keep out the rain
while there's barely room to lie on my paltry couch.
Don't be surprised if now I'm thin and drawn –
having lots of worries really gets you down.

82.

Why do I forever feel disheartened?
Life comes and goes like morning mushrooms.
Unbearable that in these twenty or thirty years
old friends and family have perished, every one.
Thinking of this I'm stricken with grief,
moved by unendurable sorrow.
What is there to do – what can I do?
Devote myself to being a mountain recluse.

## III. LAZY AND SELFISH PEOPLE

83.

The woman was remiss about the weaving,
the man lazy about hoeing the fields,
his frivolous mind addicted to shooting a bow,
her slippers skipping as she played her strings.
But clothes are urgently needed for frozen bones
and to fill your stomach food's what matters most.
Now whose sympathies do you have
as you cry in anguish to the dark blue sky?

84.

We call them devout old ladies, but their devotions
are to the depraved rather than the Way.
They don't express much remorse to god or Buddha
but harbour plenty of jealous thoughts.
They guzzle fish and meat behind your back
while intoning the name of the Buddha to your face.
If this is how they manage self-cultivation
they'll find it hard to avoid the river to hell.

The Way (Dao) here is the Buddhist way. The river is named
here as the Nai he or No-Remedy River. In old Buddhist belief
the river, like the Styx, was the frontier to hell.

85.

There's a fellow whose surname is Insolence,
his given name Greedy, his courtesy name Corrupt.
As an individual he understands nothing at all;
others suspect him in everything he does.
His loathing of death is as bitter as goldthread root,
as sweet as white honey his affection for life.
He hasn't yet had enough of dining on fish
and is even less sated when it comes to meat.

A courtesy name or *zi* was one for use outside the family.
Goldthread is a plant with bitter medicinal roots.

86.

When he was young, Master Dong
went out and about in the imperial city
wearing a jacket of gosling yellow
and carrying himself like someone in a painting.
The horse he rode had snow-white hooves
and sent the dust flying as he went by.
Onlookers filled the sides of the road –
'That fellow – who can he be?'

'That fellow – who can he be?'
He was somebody roundly loathed,
foolish in heart and mind, always excited,
his unenlightened vision a drunken blur.
When he saw a Buddha he didn't pray;
meeting a monk he didn't give him alms.
He only knew how to tackle a chunk of meat –
otherwise he couldn't do a thing.

87.

I have seen people in our time
who like to carry themselves with a haughty air
but don't repay the kindness of their parents –
what kind of heart do such people have?
They borrow others' money without regrets,
at least until they're reborn as beasts of burden.
Every one of them loves his wife and children
while failing to look after his father and mother.
As for his brothers, they seem to be his enemies,
his heart and mind always resenting them.
Remember, once these people were very young
and the gods were asked to bring them up well.
Now they've grown into disrespectful sons –
the world has many people of this kind.
When they eat meat they scoff it all themselves,
wiping their mouth and saying 'I'm satisfied!'
They praise themselves and say some clever things
showing they're the smartest person around.
Not till the ox-headed guardians of hell
glare in rage do they know their time is up.
They burn good incense for a Buddha of their choice
and select a suitable monk to look after,
but if an enlightened being begs at their gate
they chase him away as an idle bonze,
unaware that those skilled in the art of doing nothing
never assume a particular form.

They write in prayer to distinguished monks,
donating two or three kinds of cash as alms;
but if Yunguang was so good at teaching the dharma
why was he reborn with horns on his head?
If your heart and mind don't treat things equally
none of the saints and sages will come to you.
The wise are mixed up together with ordinary people
and I urge you, sirs, not to choose between the two.
Our dharma, unfathomably sublime,
is what the divinities all turn towards.

The monk Yunguang once wilfully disobeyed the rules of
fasting and so was reborn as an ox. Dharma is here the
Buddhist teachings.

## IV. BEING RICH AND BEING POOR

88.

The old lady in the house to the east
has grown rich in the last few years.
Previously she was poorer than I was;
now she laughs that I have no money.
She laughs at me for falling behind;
I laugh at her for getting ahead.
We laugh at each other as if we won't stop
from the east and then from the west.

89.

Wealthy people bustle about a lot,
finding it hard to assent as things come up.
If the rice in their granary is turning red
they still won't sell an ounce to anyone.
Then again, they harbour scheming thoughts,
choosing fine silk before buying the cheaper kind.
When it comes to their demise
their mourners are the flies.

90.

I once observed an intelligent man,
learned and talented beyond compare.
Shining in official exams, he gained worldwide
     renown,
his five-word lines of verse the finest of anyone's.
Better than his peers at enlightened governance,
there was just nobody else who could take his place.
Then suddenly, with riches and rank, a taste for
     wealth and women,
the tiles broke, the ice melted – the story can't be
     told.

Writing poetry in five-character lines was part of the state
examination for prospective Tang officials.

92.

Mr Zou's wife with her downcast eyes
and Du's mother with her graceful walk
are women of the same age
with the same love of face.
Yesterday they met at a reception;
being poorly dressed they were put at the back
and just because they wore threadbare skirts
they ate other people's leftover cakes.

Hanshan describes Du's mother as coming from Handan, a
town whose people were well-known for their graceful style of
walking and singing.

93.

Away in the distance, as far as the eye can see,
white clouds are shrouded in mist all around.
Owls and crows are comfortably well-fed
while starving phoenixes range to and fro.
Splendid horses are put out to rocky shoals
while lame donkeys get into the great halls.
Questions can't be asked of heaven on high;
on the dark blue waters sits a wren.

In this poem Hanshan echoes the ancient *Songs of the South*,
with their theme of talent and integrity being overlooked.
Here fat birds and donkeys prosper while fine horses and
phoenixes suffer neglect. A solitary wren cannot challenge
such injustices.

94.

Now I have a coat —
it isn't fine or decorated silk.
If you ask what colour it is
it isn't red and isn't purple either.
In the summer I wear it as a shirt;
in the winter I use it to cover my bed.
Winter and summer, turn and turn about,
it's all I have the whole year round.

In *The Analects* Confucius remarked that red or purple were
special colours, not to to be worn casually. Hanshan's coat
was no doubt dyed the rough dark colour typical of Buddhist
monks' clothing.

95.

So many different kinds of human being,
calculating dozens of ways to get wealth and fame,
avidly setting their hearts on finding glory,
working at contriving riches and rank.
Their hearts and minds don't rest for an instant,
rushing headlong like a swirling fog.
Their family members are all around them,
so they just call out and dozens reply 'Yes sir!'
But by the time they get to seventy
the ice melts and the tiles break up.
Once dead, their affairs are all gone –
who will be in line to take them on?
If you soak a pellet of mud in water
you will see how unwise all this is.

Archers used mud, stone or metal pellets as shot. Mud pellets
broke up when wet.

96.

Greedy people love amassing wealth
just as the owl loves her youngsters.
When the owlets grow up they eat their mother;
when wealth abounds it destroys its owner.
Disperse your wealth and good fortune will be yours;
collect it and misfortunes will arise.
Do without wealth and without misfortune
and beat your wings in the deep blue clouds.

It was (mistakenly) believed that once they'd grown up owls
ate their mothers.

97.

Deep in distress, all the poor scholars
suffer cold and hunger in the extreme.
When they're idle they love to write poems,
arduously applying themselves to their work.
But who's going to notice their lowly words? –
I urge you, good sirs, to stop your sighing.
If you put your writings on sesame cakes
and feed them to dogs, they'll turn them down.

98.

A poor donkey stands short by a foot;
a wealthy dog is an extra three inches high.
Helping the poor doesn't level things up;
halving wealth brings about hardship too.
Start with the donkey getting enough to eat
and the upshot'll just be that the dog starves.
For your sake I've given this some thought
and it's left me feeling quite out of sorts.

99.

Many are the cold and hungry travellers –
born as humans, distinct from other creatures,
yet forever sheltering under millstones
or crying now and then beside the road.
For days on end they dream in vain of food;
in winter they don't think of having a coat,
simply taking along a bundle of straw
together with a few ounces of bran.

A millstone offered not just shelter but also bits of fallen grain
to eat.

100.

Who's the straitened scholar that often comes
to check the exam results at the Southern Court?
He must be around thirty years old or so
and has been a candidate four or five times.
There isn't any cash in his bag
and his satchel just holds some books.
He passes in front of a food stall
but doesn't dare for an instant to turn his head.

A candidate, that is, for the imperial exams to select officials.

101.

Distant relatives crowd round the rich and noble
just because they have the money and the grain.
The poor and lowly have families that stay away
but not because they are short of brothers.
You need to get moving and come back home –
the Lodge for Summoned Worthies isn't open yet,
and aimlessly walking Vermilion Bird Street
is wearing out the soles of your leather shoes.

Vermilion Bird Street was the main street in the capital
Chang'an. If you weren't wealthy and well-connected it
wasn't worth waiting around there for a government job. The
Lodge for Summoned Worthies was once a place for housing
respected scholar-officials.

102.

He's a poised, fine-looking young man,
learned in all the classics and histories.
He's addressed as teacher everywhere;
everybody calls him a scholar.
He hasn't yet secured an official position
and doesn't know how to hold a plough.
In winter he wraps himself in a torn cloth gown –
I'm afraid his books have led him astray.

103.

In the days when I had money
I was always lending you some.
Now you're well-fed and warm
when you see me you won't give me any.
You should recall how you wanted it once
just as I'm hoping for some now.
Having, not having – these things take turns;
do give this some careful thought.

104.

In times gone by I was getting on for poor
but today I am really poor and cold.
Nothing I am doing is going right –
I keep encountering hardships all round.
I frequently lose my footing walking in mud
and my gut often aches when I serve at village
    shrines.
I've lost my tabby cat, and the rats
are circling the storage jar for rice.

Twice a year monks prayed to the gods at village shrines and
joined the feast that followed.

105.

You may have a quite outstanding spirit
and be most refined in appearance,
be able to shoot through seven layers of armour
and read five lines of writing at a time,
have slept with a tiger's head as a pillow
and sat once on a bed of ivory,
but without that whatever-it's-called
you'll feel just as cold as the frost.

'whatever-it's-called': money. A high-minded man once
refused to mention money by name, referring to it only as
'whatever-it's-called'.

106.

You laugh at me as a simple farmer,
looking rather rough,
my headscarf never high enough,
the sash round my waist always tight.
It's not that I don't go with the times –
just that I can't afford to keep up.
One day when I have the money
I'll put up a pagoda on a mountain top.

Pagodas were the tallest and most revered structures, so
putting one on top of a mountain would be a fine way of
outdoing others.

## V. SPRING DAYS AND OTHER DIVERSIONS

107.

I'm a maiden living in Handan –
the songs I sing have a lilting tone.
Stay here in this dwelling of mine;
these melodies always last a long time.
Now you're drunk don't talk of going back,
but linger here – the day is not yet done.
I have a place for you to spend the night,
embroidered quilts spread on a silver bed.

108.

In the third month when the silkworms are small
the women come and pick the blossoms,
playing with butterflies at a bend in the wall,
casting pebbles at frogs by the water's edge.
They store up plums in their silken sleeves
and use gold hairpins to dig up bamboo shoots,
competing to see who can find the most things –
'This place wins out over mine!'

Competing to see who could gather the most new kinds of
flower or plant was a common game.

109.

Calling to each other they pick the lotuses –
such a delight, there on the clear river.
Playing together they're impervious to the dusk
though now and again they see a strong wind stir.
The waves scoop up a mandarin duck and drake
and rock a pair of purple ducks to and fro.
During this time they stay on their boat,
perpetually feeling the surge and swell.

110.

If there's wine, invite people for a drink –
if there's meat, call them in for a meal!
Sooner or later we're bound for the Yellow Springs
and have to try our hardest while we're young.
Jade belts are splendid for a while,
and golden hairpins are graceful, but not for long.
As for old Mr Zhang and old lady Zheng,
there won't be any news of them once they're gone.

This poem is unusually accepting of meat-eating. The Yellow
Springs are the realm of the dead. Zheng and Zhang are
invented names.

111.

Plenty of young women in Luoyang
display their beauty during the days of spring.
Together they pick flowers by the roadside
and stick them into their piled-up hair.
Their hair's piled high and arrayed with flowers
and if you look they all cast sidelong glances.
But don't go seeking the bitter pleasures of love –
they'll be going home to see their spouses.

Luoyang was the secondary capital of the Tang.

112.

In the spring a woman shows off her looks,
walking with friends on the path south of the field.
As she looks at the blossoms, the late sun
    troubles her
and she shelters from the wind behind some trees.
A young man comes up from the side,
riding a white horse with a golden bridle.
'Why must you flirt with me for so long?
My husband is going to know.'

113.

Going down the mountain for a while
I cross the moat into the city
where I come across a group of women,
refined and beautiful in appearance,
their hair decked with flowers in Shu style,
their faces powdered with rouge,
wearing gold bracelets inlaid with silver petals
and soft silks done in crimson and purple.
Their blushing faces have an ethereal glow
and the scent of their sashes fills the air.
People there all sneak looks at them,
falling prey to infatuated feelings,
saying 'They're like nothing in the world –
I'll go after them shadow and soul.'
A dog gnawing a dried-out bone
licks its chops, but to no avail.
People don't see that they should reflect
on what distinguishes them from beasts.
The women will turn into white-haired ladies,
growing gnome-like as they get old.
Eternally having the heart and mind of a dog
won't get you to a place free of desire.

The hairstyles of Shu, present-day Sichuan province, were the
fashion in Tang times.

114.

Among the flowers the golden orioles
are calling out their captivating songs.
A beautiful girl, her countenance like jade,
responds with the sound of strings.
She never has enough of these playful delights,
such are the tender joys of being young.
Then the flowers fly and the birds scatter
and in the autumn wind she sheds tears.

## VI.  FRIENDSHIP AND LOVE

115.

I'm used to living in a secluded place
but now and then I go to Guoqing monastery,
sometimes calling on Master Fenggan
and often going to see Mr Shide.
Then I go back up to Cold Cliff on my own,
without a like-minded person to talk to there.
I'm searching for a river that has no source –
a source may end, but this river has no end.

Fenggan and Shide (called just De in the original here), were
reputed to be Hanshan's closest companions. This is the only
time Hanshan mentions them in his poems.

116.

I've been on Cold Mountain quite a while,
staying on here for thirty years.
Yesterday I visited some dear friends –
most of them gone to the Yellow Springs,
gradually fading away, candles burned out,
forever moving on like a river's flow.
Faced this morning with my lonely shadow
I found myself shedding streams of tears.

The Yellow Springs are the realm of the dead.

117.

The weeping willows are as dark as smoke;
the flying blossoms swirl like the snow.
The husband stays in a region far from his wife
and she is somewhere thinking about him,
the two of them at either end of the sky –
when will they get to meet again?
He sends word to her, up in her moonlit room:
'Be sure not to harbour a pair of swallows.'

A pair of swallows symbolized a loving couple; he seems to be
urging her not to harbour a swallow's nest in case it reminds
her of their love for each other.

118.

When an old gentleman marries a young woman
the woman finds his white hair hard to put up with,
and when an old lady marries a young man
the man isn't enamoured of her sallow face.
But when an old gentleman marries an old lady
neither one separates from the other,
and when a young woman marries a young man
they look adoringly at one another.

119.

Last night I dreamt I went back home
and saw my wife working at her loom.
She stopped the shuttle as if preoccupied
then lifted it as if she had no strength.
When I called her she turned her head to look
but didn't recognize me.
We must have been apart for many years –
the hair on my temples isn't the colour it was.

120.

I aim to be like those who follow the Way
and frequently take them as my friends.
Sometimes I meet people freed of all troubles,
and often I welcome guests who talk about Zen.
During moonlit nights we discuss the profound,
looking into its principles till dawn comes.
Only by wiping out a myriad contrivances
do you recognize your original self.

## VII. FOOLS AND WRONGDOERS

121.

I've seen the daughter of the house to the east –
she's about eighteen years old.
The households to the west compete for her,
wanting her as a wife for their son.
They cook up sheep and a host of living things,
coming together to do such shameless killing
and laughing in delight with beaming faces
that'll cry out when they suffer punishment.

Punishment: retribution for slaughtering sentient beings.

122.

Farmers with plenty of mulberries and gardens,
their cowsheds and tracks milling with cattle –
of course they don't give credit to cause and effect,
but one day the idea'll get through their stubborn
    hides.
They'll see at first hand how everything wastes
    away –
how facing that, people all fend for themselves,
wearing trousers made of paper or pieces of tile
and in the end freezing and starving to death.

123.

In these times there's a kind of fool
who's befuddled just like a donkey.
While he may understand human speech
he has the greed and lust of a pig.
He's perilous beyond measure
and turns what's true into lies.
Is there anyone who can tell him
he isn't allowed to live here?

124.

Leaving your home thousands of miles behind you
you raise your sword and attack the Xiongnu.
If you gain the advantage the enemy will die;
if you fail to do so you'll meet your death.
His death is not to be pitied, but as for yours
what wrongdoing will have brought it about?
I'll teach you a hundred ways to win a war:
the best plan is to do without desire.

The Xiongnu were an early people to the north of China, and
its perennial enemy.

125.

You're an ignoramus to bury your head
and devote yourself to benighted demons' caves.
I keep urging you, cultivate the Way right away
but in your foolish heart and mind you're bemused.
Not being prepared to listen to what I say,
you steadily add to the flow of your evil karma.
It won't be till your head's severed from your body
that you'll know what a wretched thing you are.

Karma: the consequences of past actions for future fate
and lives.

126.

Worthy people aren't avaricious
but fools love smelting metal for gold.
Their wheatfields occupy other families' land;
the bamboo gardens are all theirs as well.
They strain their muscles in their quest for wealth
and drive their poor horses on with gritted teeth.
They should look beyond the city walls
at the graves beneath the cypresses and pines.

127.

I've seen a dim-witted person
who lives with several wives.
They've brought up eight or nine sons,
all easy-come easy-go types.
There's a new levy for frontier troops,
and he isn't as wealthy as he was.
If you fit bitter cork straps to a donkey's tail
it'll soon know that hardship follows behind.

Hardship for them follows behind, of course, in both time
and space.

128.

The new grain isn't yet ripe
while the old's already used up,
so I go and ask people for a measure or two.
I stand outside their gates, unsure of myself.
The husband comes out and tells me to ask his wife;
the wife comes out and sends me to ask her husband.
Begrudging help to someone in need –
being well off has made them into fools.

129.

In our times there's a certain kind of person
who's block-headed like a log of wood.
When he speaks he understands nothing,
saying 'I don't have a care in the world'.
Ask about the Way – he doesn't get it;
ask about the Buddha – he's not seeking him.
Consider this carefully and you'll see
how immensely troubling it is.

130.

In the north of the city old Mr Zhong
had a home with plenty of meat and wine.
When old Zhong's wife died
mourners filled his main hall.
But when old Zhong himself passed away
not a single person grieved for him.
Having dined on his wine and sliced meats,
how come these people were so cold-hearted?

131.

Life and death are predetermined;
heaven is the source of wealth and honour.
This is what an ancient said –
I'm not telling you anything misleading.
The intelligent are prone to a short life,
whereas foolish people live to an old age.
Dumb types build up a fortune
while clever people are penniless.

The first two lines are almost a direct quote from *The Analects* of Confucius.

132.

I often hear of great officers of state,
capped with red and purple pins and tassles,
their wealth and rank taking so many forms,
their love of glory knowing no shame.
Servants and horses crowd their residences;
their storage rooms are full of silver and gold.
Each of them briefly enjoys his foolish fortune,
imperviously creating his hell to come.
Suddenly he dies, his many affairs at an end,
and his sons and daughters mourn by his side,
unaware of the calamity they're facing,
how quickly they'll go down the road ahead.
The family breaks apart, cold and bleak,
without a single grain of rice to eat,
freezing and hungry, suffering bitterly –
and all because he lacked enlightenment.

The 'hell to come': the retribution he will suffer for his
worldly greed.

133.

The hearts and minds of the finest are keen –
As soon as they're told, they comprehend the
    sublime.
The hearts and minds of the middle ranks are
    pure –
they think it over and see it's a weighty affair.
But the lowest sort – they are the foolish ones,
their stubborn hides really hard to crack.
Only when their heads are dripping with blood
do they start to know what self-destruction is.
Take a look at the unrepentant thief,
executed in the crowded marketplace,
his corpse swept aside like dirt –
at that time who's he going to talk to?
Young men, fine fellows,
beheaded with a slice of the blade –
human outside, bestial within,
when will their baleful deeds come to an end?

134.

I have six brothers, older and younger
and one of them was a wicked one.
Beating him didn't have any effect
and cursing him brought no results.
There was nothing whatever to be done,
addicted as he was to wealth, sex and slaughter.
When he saw what he liked he fell for it blindly,
his greed even greater than a demon's.
Father couldn't bear to look at him
and mother was greatly displeased.
So not long ago I got hold of him
and dressed him down for his dissolute ways.
I pushed him off to a place we had to ourselves
and addressed myself to him, point by point.
'Now you'd better change your ways,' I told him,
'set right your upturned cart and take a new track.
If you don't trust me on this, I'm afraid
your evil habits will be the death of you.
But if you take this advice of mine
you and I will find a way to get by.'
Since then he's been completely amiable
and now he's even better than a saint.

He's worked hard at learning the smelting trade,
and has smelted three mountains' worth of iron.
To this day he has been at peace
and everybody's full of his praise.

Hanshan describes the demon and saint in Buddhist terms as
a *rakshasa* and a bodhisattva. The slaughter he refers to is the
slaughter of animals for food. It's been suggested that this poem is
an allegorical account of the six Buddhist sense organs (eyes, ears,
nose, tongue, body and mind) and how they can be tamed.

## VIII. GROWING OLD

135.

Behind the beaded curtains in the jade hall
there is a woman of outstanding beauty,
finer in appearance than an immortal
with features as enticing as peach or plum.
In the homes to the east, spring mists gather;
in houses to the west, the autumn wind stirs.
Thirty years from now she'll be reduced
to the residue left over from sugarcane.

136.

In the city there lives an elegant beauty,
her waist adorned with tinkling beads and jades,
playing with parrots, framed by the blossoms,
plucking at a lute by the light of the moon.
For three days her long songs resonate;
thousands watch her perform her short dances.
But things surely won't be like this forever –
lotus flowers don't last through the cold.

137.

You who are wise, you have cast me aside;
You who are foolish, I've done the same to you.
I'm not a fool but I'm not wise either
so from now on let's not stay in touch.
When night falls I'll sing by the light of the moon;
as day breaks I'll dance with the white clouds.
Not for me, being silent with folded hands,
stiffly seated, my hair in wispy curls.

138.

On a bay horse, a coral whip in hand,
he gallops through the streets of Luoyang,
full of himself, a fine-looking youth
who doesn't believe in growing old.
But the day will come when his hair turns white,
and his rosy complexion surely won't keep for good.
Just take a look at Mount Mang –
that's where the Penglai Islands are.

The Penglai Islands were said to be the home of the
immortals. Mount Mang was the site of a famous graveyard.

139.

A group of women play in the evening sun,
an incoming breeze filling the path with scent.
Their skirts are stitched with golden butterflies,
their chignons pinned by jade mandarin ducks;
the maids' pigtails are knotted with red gauze
and purple brocade laces the eunuchs' robes.
Watching them, someone has lost his way,
white hair at his temples, uneasy in heart and mind.

140.

I remember in the days of my youth
going out hunting by the Tomb of Peace,
when I didn't want to be a state official,
and wasn't yet ready to praise the immortals.
Flying along astride my white horse
I'd shout out 'Hare!' and let my eagle loose.
I wasn't aware of the great decline to come –
with my white hair, who will care about me?

The Tomb of Peace or Ping ling was the Han emperor Zhao's
tomb north-west of the capital, and a fashionable place to go.

141.

If people are always meeting their daily needs
and begrudging what they have to spend,
when they get old they won't do as they want
and others will gradually push them aside.
Once you're consigned to a grave in the wilds
the ambitions of a lifetime come to nought.
When the sheep are gone you stop mending the pen
and lost hopes endure forever more.

142.

Fold upon fold of cloud-capped mountains touch
    the sky;
the path is hidden, the forest deep, no one passes by.
Far off you see the bright light of the lonely moon;
close by you hear the birds chattering in flocks.
The old man lives on his own by the dark cliffs,
at ease in his cottage, not caring his hair is white.
He sighs at the fact that the day and the years
    gone by
have passed insensibly like the river flowing east.

143.

There are people who dread having white hair
and are loath to give up the scarlet sash of office.
They gather herbs in a vain search for immortality,
digging up roots and shoots in a random way.
For several years they achieve no results;
stupefied, they take on a frustrated glare.
You people are hunters dressed in monks'
    cassocks –
basically those aren't the things for you.

144.

After a century or so I'm old and frail —
sallow-faced, white-haired, loving the mountain life.
I wrap myself in a cloth robe and go with my destiny,
with no respect for the devious ways of people in
    the world.
They use up heart, mind and spirit for fame and
    gain,
driven on by a hundred kinds of greed.
This floating life's an illusion, like the snuff of a
    lamp;
when your body's laid in the grave that's all there is.

Some sources treat this as two poems, or leave out the
second part.

145.

I've heard that on Tiantai Mountain
there's a jade tree for immortals.
I have always wanted to climb it
but don't know where the Stone Bridge path is.
This has left me feeling melancholy
as I live alone into my twilight years.
Today I looked in the mirror
at my ageing strands of white hair.

Stone Bridge was a high, narrow path, which (as Hanshan
writes here) led to a sacred tree.

146.

Our life in this troubled dusty world
is just like the life of an insect in a bowl
which goes round and round the whole day
but can't escape the bowl it's caught in.
We can't become immortals
and suffer incalculable troubles.
Time passes like a flowing river
and in no time we grow old.

147.

Seventy years on, I went back today
to a place I used to spend time in.
Longstanding friends didn't come by –
they were interred in old burial mounds.
Now my hair's turned white, while I still have
a stretch of mountain up in the clouds,
I say to those who are coming after me,
why not study the wise words of old?

148.

Among the layered cliffs
the light breeze is enough
to let cool air pass through
without the wave of a fan.
A bright moon shines
through a cover of white cloud.
I sit here by myself,
old man that I am.

## IX. THE TRANSIENCE OF LIFE

149.

'When seeing off the dead,' said Master Zhuang,
'take their coffin to be the earth and sky.'
When my time comes, and it will,
I'll need a bamboo mat and nothing more.
Once I'm dead I'll be feeding the flies,
not troubling white cranes to mourn for me.
For those who starve on Shouyang Mountain
life is frugal, and death's a pleasure too.

The Daoist philosopher Master Zhuang (Zhuang zi) said this
on his deathbed. Cranes were associated with immortality,
and said to carry off immortals on their backs. Shouyang
Mountain was where in ancient times two high officials went
to renounce the world, eating wild grasses to survive.

150.

I spur my horse past the desolate city wall,
a desolate wall that stirs this traveller's heart –
high and low its parapets of old,
large and small its graves of long ago,
with trembling shades of lonely tumbleweed
amid the stately music of mighty trees.
Sadly these are all the bones of common folk,
none named in the annals of the immortals.

'common folk': here, lay people.

151.

There's no rest for the four seasons —
as one year goes, so another arrives.
In the world of things the new replaces the old,
all except for the heavens, which never decay.
As the east grows light the west is turning dark;
with every flower that falls another blooms.
Only the guests of the Yellow Springs
go in obscurity, never to return.

The Yellow Springs: the realm of the dead.

152.

Writings of great breadth and depth
and a quite outstanding talent,
but a life limited by its mortal span
and in death a ghost without renown:
since long ago, things have often been thus –
why do you struggle against them now?
You could come up to the white clouds
and I could teach you the Purple Mushroom Song.

The purple mushroom was a plant associated with virtue
and immortality.

153.

The splendid young man astride his horse
points with his whip to the houses of easy virtue.
As he sees it, there won't be a time for dying –
not for him a strenuous search for wisdom.
Each passing season flowers are bound to bloom
but there comes a day when they wither away.
When death is upon him he won't be able to savour
the enlightening taste of butter oil and honey.

'houses of easy virtue': referred to in the original as willows,
these being trees identified with prostitutes. 'butter oil and
honey': substances associated with the Buddha nature.

154.

Dazzling, the woman from the house of Lu,
always known by the name of Troublefree,
keen to go forth on horseback picking flowers,
happy to row out her boat to pluck lotuses.
She would sit kneeling on a green bearskin mat,
wrapping herself in dark blue phoenix furs.
Such a sadness that within a hundred years
she had to return to a mound of earth.

155.

Who'll never die, now and forever more?
Death has always dealt with us equally.
At first we think of people as standing tall,
then suddenly they become a heap of dust.
In the Yellow Springs there's no morning light;
in the spring season the grasses grow green
but when we go to our doleful place of rest
the winds in the pines sigh with mortal grief.

The Yellow Springs are the realm of the dead.

172

156.

I often feel as if drunk the whole day long
as I mourn the endless passing of the years.
Buried beneath the unkempt grasses,
under the moonlight, so dim at dawn,
flesh and bones dissolve into nothing
and people's souls wither away.
If you're chewing on an iron bit
there's no point in reading the classic of Lao.

Perhaps chewing on an iron bit refers to a fear of being reborn
as an animal. Master Lao (Lao zi) is the putative author of the
Daoist classic *Dao de jing.*

157.

Peach blossoms want to last the summer through
but the seasons press on, waiting on nothing.
I search for people from the days of the Han
but it seems there isn't one to be found.
Day after day the flowers fade away;
people change as the years go by.
There where the dust stirs today
was a great sea in times long past.

The Han dynasty came to an end in 220 CE, many centuries
before Hanshan's time.

158.

A vast expanse, the Yellow River waters,
flowing ever eastwards without cease
into a far, barely visible distance
just as all our lives eventually end.
If you want to ride on the white clouds
how are you going to grow wings?
While you still have a thick head of hair
try your hardest at whatever you do.

159.

If you want an analogy for life and death
compare the two of them to water and ice.
Water comes together and becomes ice
and ice disperses again to become water.
Whatever has died is sure to be born again;
whatever is born comes round again to dying.
As ice and water do one another no harm
so life and death, the two of them, are fine.

160.

It's a waste to climb a building that reaches the sky
and pointless to mount a tower a hundred feet high.
You may cultivate the self yet die an untimely death
or be lured into studying without securing honours.
It's no use following after the reckless young;
what's there to dislike about having white hair?
If you can't yet be as straight as an arrow,
at least avoid being as crooked as a hook.

'reckless young': Hanshan uses the term yellow beaks,
meaning fledglings. Confucius warned that fledglings were
heedless of danger and easily captured, as were older birds
that followed them.

161.

Though our span of life is less than a hundred years
we always harbour centuries' worth of sorrows.
As soon as we recover from an illness
we worry about our children and grandchildren,
looking down at the roots of new growth
and up as far as the tips of the mulberry trees.
When a scale weight dropped into the eastern sea
has sunk to the seabed – then we'll know to rest.

Only when the end of life is irreversible are we ready to die.

162.

As I went walking I passed an ancient grave
and spent my tears lamenting life and death.
The tomb was broken, crushing the coffin inside,
its yellow cypress pierced by whitened bones.
Old jars and jugs were lying on their sides;
in the jumble hatpins and tablet were gone.
A wind took hold of the centre ground,
stirring up billowing clouds of dust.

Hatpins and writing tablets were part of the paraphernalia of
any official, buried with him.

163.

Where there's pleasure to be had, take it –
now's the time! and it's not to be lost.
We talk about life spanning a century
but it never lasts thirty thousand days.
We stay a fleeting moment in the world
so don't go quarrelling over money.
The last part of *The Classic of Filial Piety*
sets out in detail how things end.

The last section of the Confucian classic on filial piety is about
loving and respecting your parents and mourning them with
due decorum when they die.

164.

I close the gate to my rustic home, but in vain –
time flashes by me, the spark from a flint.
I've only heard of people reborn as ghosts,
never seen cranes becoming immortals.
Thinking this over, what else is there to say? –
Follow your destiny, have pity on yourself.
Turn and look beyond the city walls
at the old graves ploughed into fields.

Cranes were supposed to carry away those who achieved
immortality. The last line is from the early *Nineteen
Old Poems.*

165.

I have seen the people of this world
living their lives then going back to die.
Yesterday they were still sixteen,
men sturdy in spirit, vigorous in intent.
Now they've reached seventy or so,
their strength drained, their bodies withered,
just like the blossoms of a spring day
that bloom in the morning and fall at night.

166.

Of the many wise people through the ages
none has remained here for good.
They live their lives, then return to death,
all of them transformed into dust.
Their bones are piled as high as Mount Vipala;
those they part from make a sea of tears.
All they have left behind are empty names –
ineluctable, the wheel of life and death.

Mount Vipala was a mountain in north-east India renowned
for its great height.

167.

You have seen how the flowers among the leaves
can't stay looking good for more than a while.
Today there's the fear that somebody will pick them;
tomorrow someone or other will sweep them away.
How sad it is that after the years have passed
beguiling beauty turns into old age.
Compare the world we live in to the flowers –
rosy looks are hard to keep for long.

168.

Master Hanshan
is forever thus,
dwelling on his own,
neither living nor dying.

## X. ANECDOTES

169.

Parrots live in the countries to the west
where hunters capture them and bring them here.
All day long fine ladies play with them,
coming and going in the women's quarters,
giving them gifts of gilded cages where
they are shut in – slam! – spoiling their feather
    coats.
They'd be better off as wild geese or cranes
Soaring up high into the clouds.

170.

Two turtles go for a ride in an ox cart
trotting along the road and having fun.
A scorpion comes from the side of the road
and asks them urgently to take him along.
They'll be lacking in feeling not to give him a ride
but as soon as they do they're going to be in trouble.
Snap your fingers – aha! – there can be no doubt:
an act of kindness will still get them stung.

'Snap your fingers': a gesture of amazement, excitement, etc.,
common among Buddhists.

171.

A white crane carried bitter peaches in his beak,
resting just once in a flight of a thousand miles,
his destination the mountains of Penglai,
the peaches for him to eat during his journey.
But before he arrived his feathers wilted away
so he separated in sorrow from his flock
and flew back home to his old nest –
where his mate didn't know who he was.

Penglai: eastern islands where immortals live. 'Miles' here
and later are li or Chinese miles, at this time about a third of
a western mile.

172.

The wealthy got together in a great hall,
splendidly lit by their patterned lanterns.
At the time someone without a candle
really wanted to stay there to one side.
Who'd have thought they would drive her out,
send her away to hide at home in the dark.
What harm was there in giving her some light? –
quite a surprise, begrudging some leftover rays.

173.

In a broken-down neglected hut
smoke and flames were spreading.
They asked the group of children inside
'Have you just been born?
Three carts are waiting outside the gate
ready to take you, but you won't go!'
They'd eaten their fill, their tummies bulged –
what a dim-witted lot they were.

This story is taken from the Lotus sutra.

174.

In years past I went travelling to the ocean
to get the *mani* jewel I'd sworn to secure.
Going straight to the dragon king's secret palace
I broke open its golden gates, to the chief god's
    wrath.
To protect the jewel the dragon king put it in
    his ear;
his swordsmen flashed their weapons and stopped
    my search.
So this dealer went back home, only to find
that all along the bright jewel was in my mind.

The *mani* jewel was a precious Buddhist jewel.

175.

A deer lives in the forest
drinking the water, eating the grass,
stretching out to sleep under a tree –
such a delight, life without a care.
But tether it in an elegant hall
and feed it the most sumptuous food –
for ages it won't be willing to eat
and you'll see it fade away.

## XI. OCCASIONAL REFLECTIONS ON MONKHOOD

176.

A white whisk with a sandalwood handle –
throughout the day I breathe in its fragrance.
It floats gently like a furling mist
or goes to and fro like a passing cloud.
Respectfully held, it's good for summer heat;
Lifted up high, it does away with the dust.
From time to time in the abbot's rooms
it's used to point the way for somebody lost.

Being made of prized sandalwood, the whisk was evidently
the abbot's.

177.

Naturally there are miserly people
but as for me I'm not the miserly type.
My monk's robe is good for dancing in
and I use up wine on drinking songs.
Fill your stomach up with food
and don't let your feet grow weary.
When the grass grows through your skull,
on that day, sir, you'll have your regrets.

178.

I'm going to tell you a few things –
think about them and you'll know I'm a good man.
If you're penniless hold back from selling your home;
only when you're rich should you buy a field.
If your stomach's empty don't run around;
if your head rests on a pillow don't fall asleep.
These are words that everyone should see –
hang them on the east side where the sun rises.

'if your head rests on a pillow don't fall asleep': stay alert even
when resting comfortably. 'hang them on the east side': in a
temple or monastery, perhaps.

179.

There's a smooth-skinned creature on Cold
　　Mountain
with a white body and a dark head of hair
who holds in his hand a book in two parts,
one on the Way, the other on its virtue.
There's no pot or stove where he lives
and he goes out walking without a monk's robe,
but he always carries the sword of wisdom,
ready to destroy that villainous thing, distress.

'a smooth-skinned creature': a human, that is, rather than a
furry animal. The book in two parts is the Daoist classic
*Dao de jing*. Like the sword of wisdom, distress (*kleśa*) is a
Buddhist term.

180.

Yesterday I went to the Rose Cloud Temple
and happened on some Revered Immortal
    Masters
clad in star-studded hats and moon-tinted robes
who told me all about being mountain recluses.
I asked them about the art of being immortal
to which they replied, 'It's incomparable!'
They regarded it as the supreme spirit,
a wondrous remedy, a bounden sacred secret.
They would hold on till death to await a crane,
or (as they all said) a fish to carry them off.
I went over this thoroughly in my mind
and came to the conclusion it didn't make sense.
You only need to watch an arrow shot in the air
to see how in no time it falls back to the ground.
Even if you were to become an immortal
you'd be just like a ghost holding on to a corpse.
Our hearts and minds have the brilliance of the
    moon,
not comparable to the world's myriad forms.

If you want to know the art of the elixir of life
it's the original spirit within yourself.
Don't follow the Yellow Turban Lords,
or take their foolishness as a model.

The Revered Immortal Masters were Daoist priests or monks,
one of whose aims was to make an elixir of immortality. Once
immortal they thought they would be carried off by cranes
or fishes. The name Yellow Turban Lords may refer to the
yellow of the priests' robes, and allude to early Daoist rebels
who wore yellow turbans.

181.

There's a type of person in this world
who's really enough to make anybody laugh.
He leads a monk's life, clad in tattered robes,
fooling people to think he's a man of the Way.
His clothes should be undefiled
but they're home to a number of lice.
He'd be better off going back home
and recognizing the heart and mind are fine.

## XII. MORE BUDDHIST OBSERVATIONS

182.

What a delight this good gentleman is,
cutting such an imposing figure –
not even thirty years of age
yet having such an array of talents.
On a gold-bridled horse he rides with other heroes,
gathering fine friends for a sumptuous meal.
There is only one thing wrong with him –
he doesn't pass on the lamp that never fails.

'the lamp that never fails': the wisdom of the Buddha.

183.

We sail in this boat of rotten wood,
gathering the bitter fruit of the neem tree,
and on arriving at the great sea
go with the never-ending waves,
with grain enough for a single night
and a shore three thousand miles away.
Our affliction – how does it arise?
sadly, from the suffering destiny causes.

Neem is an Indian tree with bitter leaves and fruit sometimes
associated with suffering. Affliction here refers to the
Buddhist concept *kleśa*.

184.

What's the reason for this weeping,
your tears dropping like pearls?
Either you've bid someone a last farewell
or you've suffered a catastrophic loss.
The reason you are in such dire straits
is that you can't yet grasp cause and effect.
I look with due respect at corpses by their graves,
but I'm not concerned by the six realms of rebirth.

In Buddhist belief the six realms of rebirth are those of hell,
hungry ghosts, animals, malevolent spirits, humans and
gods. The realm you are reborn into depends on karma, the
consequences of past actions.

185.

Some seek a joyful existence, hanker for it,
unaware that their century of life will end in woe.
If we just look at a mirage on rippling waves
we'll see that impermanence is our deadly bane.
If a man has a will as unbending as iron,
no crookedness in his heart, his Way intrinsically
    true,
like bamboo growing thick and tall beneath the
    frost –
only then will he know how to put his spirits to
    good use.

186.

Anger in your heart and mind is a fire
that can burn through a forest of virtues achieved.
If you're going to practise the way of the Buddha
protect your true heart and mind by being patient.

Patience: here a Buddhist ideal, *kṣānti* in Sanskrit.

187.

Bad rebirths are murky in the extreme –
deep in the darkness without any sunlight
for so long that after eight human centuries
you haven't yet reached the middle of your night.
The many foolish people of this kind
are surely in the most pitiable state,
so do seek liberation, good sirs,
by acknowledging the king of dharma.

In Buddhist belief those with bad rebirths are reborn into the
realms of hell, hungry ghosts and animals. The liberation is
from the cycle of death and rebirth. The king of dharma or
teachings is the Buddha.

188.

The sky is high, endlessly high.
The earth is deep, limitlessly deep.
We living creatures exist between the two,
relying on their transformative powers.
We fight one another for food and warmth
and calculate how to eat each other up.
We don't yet fully grasp cause and effect,
blind people asking, 'What's the colour of milk?'

189.

In our time we have some brilliant scholars
who strenuously research textual mysteries
with singular skills in inkbrush, sword and speech
and unrivalled accomplishments in the six arts.
Their vitality is extraordinarily rare,
their spirits outshining those of ordinary folk.
But they don't acknowledge the one central idea
and the realms they look into are scattered in
    disarray.

The six traditional arts were ritual, music, archery,
charioteering, calligraphy and arithmetic. The one central
idea was Buddhist belief.

190.

Limitless, the calculus of change,
never ceasing, the realms of life and death.
In a bad rebirth you could take the form of a bird
or a horned mountain cat in the five great peaks,
in corrupt times a sheep with curly hair
or in a pure age a horse that's fleet of foot.
Once long ago I was a wealthy man;
this time I've become a penniless fellow.

The five great mountains are in the north, south, east,
west and centre of China. Hanshan refers to the fleet-footed
horse as Green Ears (Lu Er), one of the legendary King Mu's
prized horses.

191.

For the hundred years of a person's life
the Buddha's teachings come in twelve parts.
Compassion is compared to a wild deer,
anger likened to a household dog.
Drive off a household dog and he won't leave
whereas a wild deer always loves to run.
To subdue your monkey heart and mind
you have to heed the roar of the lion.

The canon of Mahayana (Great Vehicle) Buddhism is
divided into twelve parts. The heart and mind are like a
monkey because they won't stay still. The lion's roar is the
commanding teaching of the Buddha.

192.

Invaluable, this heavenly thing of nature,
a thing quite on its own and all alone.
Look for it and you won't see it;
it goes in and out, but not through doors.
Compress it and it fits inside your heart;
extend it and it stretches everywhere.
If you don't accept it trustingly
when you meet it there won't be a rapport.

The natural thing is the Buddha nature.

193.

I have a cave
with nothing inside.
Spotless, emptily spacious,
it shines with a brilliant light.
A simple diet sustains a trifling frame;
a cloth robe covers an unreal form.
Let the sage appear in countless ways –
I have the Buddha of Heavenly Truth.

The sage's appearances being the many forms of the Buddha,
past, present and future. The Buddha of Heavenly Truth is the
ultimate or real Buddha.

194.

In these times there are very busy people,
widely informed, discerning in everything,
who don't acknowledge their fundamental nature
and are even further removed from the Way.
If they could understand the true reality
they wouldn't need to make empty pledges,
knowing their heart and mind through a single idea,
revealing the insights of the Buddha.

The Way here is the Buddhist way. The true reality is the
ultimate Buddhist truth.

195.

I see people in the world
blearily going down a dusty road.
Without knowing this central thing
how will they make the journey?
They can only thrive for so many days,
devoted for a while to those they love.
Even if they have a thousand catties of gold
it's still better to be poor in the woods.

This central thing: Buddhist belief.
A catty or *jin* was a measurement of weight roughly equal to
200 grams or half a pound.

196.

Let me tell you as you cultivate the Way,
search and you'll wear your spirit out in vain.
People have a pure and vital essence
for which there is no word or term.
Call it and it responds with clarity;
it doesn't dwell in obscurity.
I urge you once and again, look after it well –
don't let it have the slightest flaw.


197.

A thousand births, ten thousand deaths – how
    many lives is that?
As life and death come and go, we get increasingly
    dazed.
Not recognizing the priceless jewel in our heart
    and mind
we're like a blind donkey following its hooves.

198.

What's the most pitiful thing in the world?
The raft taking wrongdoers to the three evil
    rebirths.
They've paid no heed to this white cloud recluse
whose cold cassock comprises the shores of his life.
Let the forest shed its leaves when autumn's here
and trees bloom with the coming of the spring;
I sleep at ease in the three realms without concerns,
my home the bright moon and the clear breeze.

In Buddhism the three evil rebirths are in hell, as a hungry
ghost, or as an animal. The three realms are desire, form
and spirit.

199.

When water is crystal clear
naturally you see right to the bottom.
When your heart and mind have no concerns
the creatures lurking in clear water all appear.
If no delusions arise in your heart and mind
they'll remain unchanged for an eternity.
If you can understand things in this way
there won't be two sides to what you know.

200.

In the boundless waters of the ocean
great multitudes of creatures of the deep
take it in turns to consume each other's
benighted and dumb mortal flesh.
Unless our hearts and minds cut off delusions
deluded thoughts rise up like a mist.
If the moon of our true nature shines clear
it will cast its light far and wide, without end.

201.

Such an abundance of treasures,
carried at sea on a broken-down ship
whose bow has lost its mast
and whose stern is without a rudder.
It twists and turns, blown by the winds,
pitching up and down with the waves.
How are we to reach the other shore? –
by exerting ourselves, not just sitting tight.

202.

When Hanshan speaks out like this
he seems like a crazy fellow.
If something's up, he's forthright,
and that's enough to make others hate him.
But his heart and mind are true, and he talks
    straight –
a straight heart and mind, nothing two-faced.
When others die and cross the river to hell
who will be the clever fellows then,
as in the dark they take the shadowy road,
tethered by their karma?

203.

Wretched, those born into this floating world
in eternal flux – when will it ever end?
Day in, day out they have no time to rest,
oblivious of growing old year by year.
Their constant search for food and clothing
brings distress to their hearts and minds,
turmoil they've endured for thousands of years,
to and fro on the three evil paths of incarnation.

The three evil paths of reincarnation are being reborn as
animals or hungry ghosts or in hell.

## XIII. MISCELLANEOUS VERSES

204.

There's a use for everything,
and each has a use it's suitable for.
If it isn't used in the right place
it'll be defective, lacking what's required.
Sadly, it's quite pointless to make
a square peg for a round hole.
As for catching mice, a fine steed
won't be as good as a lame cat.

205.

I saw a very large pack of dogs,
all of them with bristling fur.
Those lying about did so as they pleased;
those running around ran that way too.
But when I tossed them a bone
they fell to snarling and scrapping,
basically because a pack of dogs
won't share a few bones equally.

206.

If you come across a baleful spirit
the main thing is, don't be afraid.
Be resolute and pay it no attention;
call out its name and it'll be sure to go.
Light incense and seek the power of the Buddha,
say a prayer and ask for the help of a monk.
If a mosquito bites an iron ox
there's nowhere for it to sink its teeth.

There was an old belief that if you knew a ghost's name and
said it, it would go.

207.

Pigs eat dead people's flesh;
people eat dead pigs' guts.
Pigs are not averse to humans' stench;
for their part people say pig has a fragrant smell.
When pigs die we toss them into the river;
when people die we bury them in the earth.
If both of them stopped eating one another
lotus flowers would grow in boiling water.

208.

We were happy in our primeval frame –
it meant we didn't eat or urinate.
Then some being drilled us with holes
as a result of which we have nine orifices.
We work day in, day out for food and clothes,
troubled about our taxes year after year.
A thousand people fight for a piece of cash,
piling in and shouting for their life.

209.

Even if you store up rhino horns
or wear a belt made with tiger's eyes,
use peach tree branches to ward off unclean spirits
or make a necklace out of garlic cloves,
drink dogwood wine to warm your stomach
and cleanse your heart with wolfberry soup,
in the end there's no avoiding death –
no point in looking for eternal life.

---

Rhino horns, tiger's eyes, peach tree branches and garlic were
all thought to dispel evil spirits, and dogwood and wolfberry
to have health-giving properties.

210.

Some take the stinking sumac tree
and call it white sandalwood.
Countless people study the Way
but few of them attain nirvana.
They discard gold and shoulder weeds instead,
deceiving others and also deceiving themselves.
It's like collecting sand in one spot
to make into a ball – a very hard thing to do.

211.

Steaming sand with the aim of making rice
or starting to dig a well when you're thirsty
or strenuously grinding away at a brick
even though that won't make a mirror –
The Buddha says that while originally equal,
everything has its eternally real nature;
so just do some careful self-reflection –
there's no use in striving pointlessly.

212.

They scrutinize the affairs of the world
and have a detailed knowledge of them all.
Whatever the affair, they're not easy to deal with,
entirely devoted to getting what suits them.
They protect themselves by making the rotten good,
slander others by turning right into wrong.
So I'm aware that the great medley of voices
always follows them behind my back.
I measure cool and warm for myself,
not believing what other wretches say.

213.

There's no need to attack others' failings
and it's no use boasting of your merits.
When you're to come out, you can do so;
when you're to withdraw, you can do so too.
Get well paid and you'll be stressed by heavy duties;
confide in friends and you'll worry they'll let you
    down.
If you pay heed to all this and remember it,
those coming after will see for themselves.

This echoes a saying of Confucius in *The Analects*: 'come out
when needed, hide when you're set aside'.

214.

When I was young and lived with my older brothers,
I'd take a classic to read as I hoed the fields.
The others told me off, and what's more
my own wife distanced herself from me.
So I cut myself off from the dusty world
and roamed round reading books as I love to do.
Who can fetch a ladleful of water
to revive this fish floundering in a rut?

In the Daoist classic *Zhuang zi*, it's told that a fish floundering in a rut asked the Daoist master Zhuang zi for a ladleful of water. The great man offered to divert a river, but the fish said a ladleful of water would do, otherwise he'd end up in a dried fish shop.

215.

Whose is this impressive wineshop
with its full-bodied wines,
its banners hoisted delightfully high,
its measures fair to the sharpest eye?
And why, to my surprise, does it do no sales?
The family have a bevy of fierce dogs
so when young servants come along to buy
the dogs bite them and they run away.

216.

Ah, this degenerate world of ours
where demons mingle with worthy men.
Some say the two are of the same ilk –
so how do we know their Ways are not akin?
When a fox pretends to have the strength of a lion
we call deception a precious thing.
But lead must be put in a smelting oven
before we find out that its gold isn't real.

217.

The man is in such a frantic hurry –
divining a spot to live needs really looking into.
Diseases are common in the south;
in the north there are bitter winds and frosts.
You can't live in the wild frontier regions
where poisonous water isn't fit to drink.
Oh wandering soul, come back home!
and enjoy the mulberry fruit in my garden.

'Oh . . . soul, come back' echoes the archaic language of the old
*Songs of the South*.

218.

Here's a fellow who looks to be in good shape
and is thoroughly conversant with the six arts.
See him in the south and he's speeding back north;
meet him in the west and he's rushing to the east.
Like duckweed he's forever floating around,
tumbleweed that doesn't stay in one place.
You may ask, what kind of person is this?
His name is Needy, his family name Poorman.

The six traditional arts were ritual, music, archery,
charioteering, calligraphy and arithmetic.

219.

The pettiness of common folk is truly petty
even if each of us differs in heart and mind.
Old Mr Yin laughs at old Liu
and old Liu laughs at old Mr Yin.
Why do the two of them laugh at each other
when they're both up to the same devious tricks?
If loaded carts compete on a mountain pass
and a load rolls over, it's a disaster for both.


220.

How many people on Tiantai
don't acknowledge Master Hanshan.
They don't get his true meaning,
calling what he says idle talk.

221.

While you're alive don't go visiting people;
do without 'kindness' and 'justice' till you die.
Once you have spoken, things branch off
and your feelings are led astray.
If they create even a small deviation
it'll be the cause of great falsehood.
False words build ladders to the clouds;
cut down, they break into tiny pieces.

This poem has a strongly Daoist flavour. The first two lines
derive from the Daoist classic *Dao de jing*, which argues
that contented people have no need to go to and fro, while
kindness and justice are superfluous moral precepts. In
ancient military strategy cloud ladders were siege ladders.

222.

You surely don't avoid death by reading books;
reading books surely won't stop you being poor.
So what's there to like in knowing the written
    word? –
by doing so you're better than other people.
If a man doesn't know the written word
there's nowhere for him to establish himself.
Like goldthread dipped in garlic sauce
deluded thinking leaves a bitter taste.

---

Illiteracy fosters bitter delusions. Chinese goldthread is a
bitter herb used as a medication.

*223.*

I've seen those who cheat other people –
it's as if they're running with a basket of water.
However speedily they take it home
the basket's bound to end up empty.
I've seen people cheated by others –
they're just like leeks in a vegetable garden.
Every day they're cut with knives
but they still keep the life intrinsic to them.

224.

When people of our time meet Hanshan,
they all say he's out of his mind.
His appearance doesn't merit a glance,
just wrapped as he is in cotton clothes.
He uses a language others don't understand,
while he doesn't speak others' language,
so he tells the people that pass by,
'You can come to Cold Mountain.'

225.

In the village where I live
people praise me as being beyond compare.
But yesterday when I went into town
even the dogs were measuring me up.
Some people complained my trousers were too
     narrow,
others talked about the length of my gown.
When you bind the eyes of a sparrowhawk
the sparrows dance about in grand style.

226.

A few foolish young people
aren't honest in what they do.
Before they've read ten chapters of a book
they grab a brush with correcting ink.
Essays on the conduct of literati
they call the rules of thieves.
They shed their skins like the silverfish
that eat away at the covers of books.

227.

In the past I was extremely poor;
night after night I counted others' treasures.
Now I've weighed this up carefully
and decided I should do business myself.
I've dug up a treasure hoard
and it comprises a crystal pearl.
There are a lot of blue-eyed foreigners
who secretly plan to buy it off me.
So I have let them know
that this pearl doesn't have a price.

228.

All my life I've been slack in what I've done,
preferring what is light to what is heavy.
While others studied for an occupation
I devoted myself to a one-chapter classic,
giving no thought to turning it into a scroll
that I'd have to carry around with me.
Prescribe the right remedy for an illness –
save humankind by suitable means.
If you just trust in yourself and have no concerns
you'll be brilliant in every way.

The classic may have been a Buddhist sutra or some other
work. Suitable means are *upāya*, a Buddhist term.

229.

In my village there's a house,
a place with no proper owner.
In the earth an inch of grass grows
and water falls as dew, drop by drop.
Fire has burned out the six thieves;
wind has blown off dark clouds and rain.
Search with care for the person there –
a perfect pearl wrapped in a cloth.

Earth, water, fire, and air or wind are the four elements. The
six senses, known to Buddhists as the six thieves, are sight,
hearing, smell, taste, touch and perception.

230.

I lived in a village
without a father or a mother,
and with no name or family position –
people just called me Zhang or Wang.
There was no one to teach me, either;
what I knew about mostly was being poor.
But I cared for myself – my heart and mind
were true and as hard as a diamond.

231.

Since being born thirty years ago
I have travelled a huge number of miles,
on rivers where green grasses abound,
on frontiers where the red dust rises.
I've concocted potions in a vain search for long life,
read the classics and recited the histories.
Today I'm coming home to Cold Mountain
to pillow my head on a stream and rinse my ears.

## XIV. ON HANSHAN'S POEMS

232.

When the dumbest sorts read my verse
they don't get it and make fun of it.
When ordinary people read my verse
they reckon it's a very weighty matter.
When outstanding people read my verse
they take it up and break into a broad smile.
Likewise when Yang Xiu saw a young woman
he knew at a glance that she was wonderful.

The scholar Yang Xiu was asked in a riddle how to describe
a young woman. At once he combined two Chinese characters
for 'young' and 'woman' to make a single character meaning
'wonderful'.

233.

Once I was on Cold Mountain my concerns were
    over —
no more worries to weigh on my heart and mind.
Idly I write poems on the rock walls,
letting my fate go with my unmoored boat.


234.

A visitor has doubts about Master Hanshan:
'Sir, your poems don't make good sense.'
'But,' say I, 'I have seen from the ancients
that there's nothing shameful in being poor.'
Laughing at these words he replies,
'What you're saying is so out of date.
I hope, sir, you'll be as we are today,
when money is all that really matters.'

235.

Five hundred pieces with five-character lines,
seventy-nine with seven-character lines,
twenty-one with three-character lines,
making six hundred poems in all,
the whole series written on cliff-face rocks –
though I say it myself, I have a good hand.
If you can understand all my poems
you really are the mother of the Buddha.

236.

Some people laugh at my poems,
but my poems are elegant enough,
and without the need of comments by Mr Zheng,
or the explanations of Mr Mao.
I have no regrets if they're rarely understood
since they're only for a few discerning friends.
If it's about not using the proper tones,
I'm at fault and lacking in talent, that's for sure.
But as they get to people with true insight
they'll spread everywhere of their own accord.

Mao and Zheng were two early commentators on the old
*Classic of Poetry*. Chinese being a tonal language, Chinese
characters in more formally structured Tang verse had to
follow prescribed sequences of tones.

237.

If your home has the poems of Hanshan
they're better for you to read than sutras.
Write them out on a screen
and look at them now and again.

# A note on the text, and a findings list

The poems in this book are listed by number. These numbers are listed below alongside the numbers of the poems concerned as found in two other English translations of Hanshan. The two translations, both rewarding works, are by Paul Rouzer (PR) and Red Pine (RP), the pen name of Bill Porter. Rouzer's numbering replicates the numbering of the poems as given in the modern Chinese edition of Hanshan collated and annotated by Xiang Chu (XC). Like earlier work by the Japanese scholar Iriya Yashitaka, Xiang's commentaries on Hanshan are invaluable, and I am enormously indebted to him. Xiang uses as his original text a Song dynasty edition of Hanshan reprinted in the huge anthology *Sibu congkan* (*The Four Branches of Literature Collection*), published in Shanghai in 1919–36. Another early anthology, *Quan Tang shi* (*Complete Tang Poems*), compiled by Cao Yin in the early eighteenth century, gives Hanshan's poems in the same sequence as Xiang's.

Red Pine provides a findings list for other English-language translations of Hanshan. There are also findings lists in two other useful English translations of Hanshan, those by Robert Henricks and by Kazuaki Tanahashi and Peter Levitt.

In this Pocket Poets edition, where the Hanshan poems are divided into fourteen topics, within each topic the poems follow the overall sequencing given in Rouzer and Xiang. The Chinese text used for this edition is the one given in Xiang, taking into account occasional textual variants as provided by him.

| THIS BOOK | PR/XC | RP | | THIS BOOK | PR/XC | RP |
|---|---|---|---|---|---|---|
| TOPIC I | | | | | | |
| 1 | 2 | 1 | | 10 | 20 | 4 |
| 2 | 3 | 3 | | 11 | 22 | 27 |
| 3 | 4 | 11 | | 12 | 24 | 29 |
| 4 | 5 | 12 | | 13 | 26 | 242 |
| 5 | 9 | 16 | | 14 | 27 | 31 |
| 6 | 10 | 17 | | 15 | 28 | 32 |
| 7 | 15 | 21 | | 16 | 30 | 34 |
| 8 | 16 | 22 | | 17 | 31 | 35 |
| 9 | 18 | 24 | | 18 | 44 | 48 |

| THIS BOOK | PR/XC | RP | | THIS BOOK | PR/XC | RP |
|---|---|---|---|---|---|---|
| 19 | 51 | 5 | | 56 | 257 | 255 |
| 20 | 66 | 69 | | 57 | 258 | 256 |
| 21 | 67 | 6 | | 58 | 261 | 259 |
| 22 | 78 | 79 | | 59 | 264 | Shide 1 |
| 23 | 81 | 82 | | 60 | 266 | 263 |
| 24 | 106 | 106 | | 61 | 267 | 264 |
| 25 | 107 | 107 | | 62 | 268 | 265 |
| 26 | 119 | 118 | | 63 | 278 | 274 |
| 27 | 130 | 133 | | 64 | 279 | 10 |
| 28 | 131 | 134 | | 65 | 283 | 278 |
| 29 | 144 | 147 | | 66 | 284 | 279 |
| 30 | 154 | 157 | | 67 | 287 | 282 |
| 31 | 155 | 158 | | 68 | 292 | 287 |
| 32 | 164 | 26 | | 69 | 295 | 290 |
| 33 | 165 | — | | 70 | 297 | 9 |
| 34 | 166 | 165 | | 71 | 306 | 300 |
| 35 | 167 | 166 | | 72 | 307 | 301 |
| 36 | 169 | 167 | | 73 | 308 | 302 |
| 37 | 171 | 169 | | 74 | 309 | 303 |
| 38 | 176 | 174 | | TOPIC II | | |
| 39 | 177 | 175 | | 75 | 32 | 36 |
| 40 | 178 | 176 | | 76 | 33 | 37 |
| 41 | 180 | 178 | | 77 | 68 | 70 |
| 42 | 183 | 181 | | 78 | 69 | 71 |
| 43 | 191 | 197 | | 79 | 145 | 148 |
| 44 | 192 | 198 | | 80 | 147 | 150 |
| 45 | 194 | 193 (part) | | 81 | 174 | 172 |
| 46 | 195 | 191 | | 82 | 251 | 249 |
| 47 | 200 | 194 | | TOPIC III | | |
| 48 | 201 | 199 | | 83 | 73 | 75 |
| 49 | 203 | 204 | | 84 | 74 | 76 |
| 50 | 206 | 207 | | 85 | 76 | 78 |
| 51 | 212 | — | | 86 | 137/8 | 140/1 |
| 52 | 216 | 213 | | 87 | 159 | 241 |
| 53 | 222 | 219 | | TOPIC IV | | |
| 54 | 227 | 224 | | 88 | 36 | 40 |
| 55 | 229 | 226 | | 89 | 37 | 41 |

| THIS BOOK | PR/XC | RP | | THIS BOOK | PR/XC | RP | |
|---|---|---|---|---|---|---|---|
| 90 | 38 | 42 | | 124 | 87 | 88 | |
| 91 | 41 | 45 | | 125 | 89 | 90 | |
| 92 | 43 | 47 | | 126 | 94 | 94 | |
| 93 | 59 | 62 | | 127 | 125 | 124 | |
| 94 | 82 | 83 | | 128 | 126 | 125 | |
| 95 | 85 | 86 | | 129 | 136 | 139 | |
| 96 | 86 | 87 | | 130 | 140 | 143 | |
| 97 | 99 | 99 | | 131 | 224 | 221 | |
| 98 | 114 | 114 | | 132 | 242 | 238 | |
| 99 | 116 | 120 | | 133 | 243 | 239 | |
| 100 | 120 | 119 | | 134 | 244 | 240 | |
| 101 | 124 | 123 | | TOPIC VIII | | | |
| 102 | 129 | 128 | | 135 | 13 | 20 | |
| 103 | 151 | 154 | | 136 | 14 | 7 | |
| 104 | 158 | 161 | | 137 | 25 | 30 | |
| 105 | 184 | 182 | | 138 | 47 | 51 | |
| 106 | 185 | 183 | | 139 | 62 | 65 | |
| TOPIC V | | | | 140 | 101 | 101 | |
| 107 | 23 | 28 | | 141 | 121 | 296 | |
| 108 | 35 | 39 | | 142 | 123 | 122 | |
| 109 | 50 | 54 | | 143 | 157 | 160 | |
| 110 | 53 | 56 | | 144 | 197 | 195 | (part) |
| 111 | 60 | 63 | | 145 | 218 | 215 | |
| 112 | 61 | 64 | | 146 | 236 | 233 | |
| 113 | 170 | 168 | | 147 | 296 | 291 | |
| 114 | 294 | 289 | | 148 | 310 | 304 | |
| TOPIC VI | | | | TOPIC IX | | | |
| 115 | 40 | 44 | | 149 | 8 | 15 | |
| 116 | 49 | 53 | | 150 | 11 | 18 | |
| 117 | 52 | 55 | | 151 | 17 | 23 | |
| 118 | 128 | 127 | | 152 | 19 | 25 | |
| 119 | 134 | 137 | | 153 | 21 | 8 | |
| 120 | 280 | 275 | | 154 | 42 | 46 | |
| TOPIC VII | | | | 155 | 46 | 50 | |
| 121 | 56 | 59 | | 156 | 48 | 52 | |
| 122 | 57 | 60 | | 157 | 55 | 58 | |
| 123 | 75 | 77 | | 158 | 64 | 67 | |

| THIS BOOK | PR/XC | RP | THIS BOOK | PR/XC | RP |
|---|---|---|---|---|---|
| 159 | 100 | 100 | 193 | 162 | 163 |
| 160 | 122 | 121 | 194 | 168 | 132 |
| 161 | 135 | 138 | 195 | 172 | 170 |
| 162 | 143 | 146 | 196 | 179 | 177 |
| 163 | 146 | 149 | 197 | 196 | 185 |
| 164 | 220 | 217 | 198 | 198 | 187 |
| 165 | 265 | 262 | 199 | 211 | 209 |
| 166 | 282 | 277 | 200 | 228 | 225 |
| 167 | 300 | 294 | 201 | 232 | 229 |
| 168 | 311 | 305 | 202 | 237 | 234 |
| TOPIC X | | | 203 | 256 | 254 |
| 169 | 12 | 19 | TOPIC XIII | | |
| 170 | 34 | 38 | 204 | 45 | 49 |
| 171 | 39 | 43 | 205 | 58 | 61 |
| 172 | 104 | 104 | 206 | 63 | 66 |
| 173 | 190 | 196 | 207 | 70 | 72 |
| 174 | 199 | — | 208 | 71 | 73 |
| 175 | 293 | 288 | 209 | 77 | 295 |
| TOPIC XI | | | 210 | 96 | 96 |
| 176 | 83 | 84 | 211 | 97 | 97 |
| 177 | 142 | 145 | 212 | 98 | 98 |
| 178 | 153 | 156 | 213 | 103 | 103 |
| 179 | 156 | 159 | 214 | 111 | 111 |
| 180 | 248 | 246 | 215 | 117 | 116 |
| 181 | 286 | 281 | 216 | 118 | 117 |
| TOPIC XII | | | 217 | 133 | 136 |
| 182 | 54 | 57 | 218 | 148 | 151 |
| 183 | 65 | 68 | 219 | 150 | 153 |
| 184 | 72 | 74 | 220 | 181 | 179 |
| 185 | 84 | 85 | 221 | 188 | 189 |
| 186 | 88 | 89 | 222 | 208 | 201 |
| 187 | 90 | 91 | 223 | 209 | 202 |
| 188 | 92 | 92 | 224 | 221 | 218 |
| 189 | 105 | 105 | 225 | 223 | 220 |
| 190 | 112 | 112 | 226 | 230 | 227 |
| 191 | 152 | 155 | 227 | 245 | 243 |
| 192 | 161 | 162 | 228 | 246 | 244 |